VISUAL GUIDE TO

Natalia Bonner

Free-Motion *Quilting* # FEATHERS

68 Modern Designs

Professional Quality Results on Your Home Machine

Joyce —
when life gives
you scraps — Quilt!
XO Natalia Bonner

stashBOOKS.

an imprint of C&T Publishing

Text copyright © 2017 by Natalia Bonner

Photography and artwork copyright © 2017 by C&T Publishing, Inc.

PUBLISHER: Amy Marson

CREATIVE DIRECTOR: Gailen Runge

EDITOR: Lynn Koolish

TECHNICAL EDITOR: Julie Waldman

COVER/BOOK DESIGNER: April Mostek

PRODUCTION COORDINATOR: Zinnia Heinzmann

PRODUCTION EDITOR: Alice Mace Nakanishi

ILLUSTRATOR: Eric Sears

PHOTO ASSISTANTS: Carly Jean Marin and Mai Yong Vang

STYLE PHOTOGRAPHY by Lucy Glover and
INSTRUCTIONAL PHOTOGRAPHY by Diane Pedersen
of C&T Publishing, unless otherwise noted

Published by Stash Books, an imprint of C&T Publishing, Inc., P.O. Box 1456,
Lafayette, CA 94549

Library of Congress Cataloging-in-Publication Data

Names: Bonner, Natalia, 1982- author.

Title: Visual guide to free-motion quilting feathers : 68 modern designs - professional
quality results on your home machine / Natalia Bonner.

Description: Lafayette, California : C&T Publishing, Inc., [2017]

Identifiers: LCCN 2016029653 | ISBN 9781617455063 (soft cover)

Subjects: LCSH: Machine quilting--Patterns. | Feathers.

Classification: LCC TT835 .B6266 2017 | DDC 646.2/1--dc23

LC record available at https://lccn.loc.gov/2016029653

Printed in China

10 9 8 7 6 5 4 3 2 1

Dedication

This book is dedicated to my mom, Kathleen Whiting. While I was writing this book, my mom, one of my best friends, was diagnosed with breast cancer. Words can never describe the feeling that comes with hearing the words, "I have cancer." My mom has been my biggest supporter throughout my career, and I can't think of a more perfect person to dedicate this book to.

Thank you so much for teaching me to sew. Thank you for letting me play with your industrial machines as a child. Thank you for dealing with me when I was such a hard teenager. Thank you for providing a space for me to quilt for several years. Thank you for being my friend. Thank you for being my biggest cheerleader.

Thank you for telling me that I can quilt feathers, because if it weren't for you, I probably wouldn't ever have fallen in love with machine quilting feathers.

Acknowledgments

Special thanks to my family for the support they provided to me on the journey of writing this book.

Thank you to Kathleen Whiting for binding my quilts; I would never have any completed quilts if it weren't for you.

Brad, thank you so much for taking care of our kids, doing all the laundry, and everything else you do to support our family so that I can put my heart and soul into my passion.

Moda Fabrics and Art Gallery Fabrics, thank you for the beautiful fabrics that you've provided for this book.

To everyone who reads my blog and attends quilt guilds with me, and to the students in my classes: your kind comments and support give more motivation and encouragement than we could have ever imagined.

To all the staff at C&T Publishing and Stash Books—thank you very much for giving me the opportunity to write this book, along with my previous four books. This journey has been so much fun, and I have enjoyed working with all of you over the past several years.

CONTENTS

Matchstick Pod
Feather   50

Diamond Pod
Feather   52

Centered
Diamond Pod
Feather   54

Double-Centered
Diamond
Pod Feather
Variation   56

Point-to-Point
Diamond
Feather   57

Point-to-Point
Feather
Variation   59

Binary Feathers   61

Simple Binary
Feather   61

Detailed
Binary Feather
Variation   62

Rotating Binary
Feather   63

Fern
Feather   64

Concave Fern
Feather   65

Hook
Feather   66

Mirrored Binary
Feather   67

Double
Half-Square
Feather   68

Capsule
Feather   71

Chic
Feather   74

Nook
Feather   76

Lateral
Feather   78

Quadrant Feathers   80

Propeller
Feather   80

Curled Propeller
Feather   81

Elongated
Feather   82

Simple Quadrant
Feather   83

Detailed
Quadrant
Feather   84

Seedling
Feather   86

Sprout
Feather   88

Simple Sprout
Feather   90

Flower and Medallion Feathers 92

Swirl Feather Flower 92

Swirl Medallion Feather 93

Sunflower Medallion Feather 94

Modern Medallion Feather 96

Square Medallion Feather 98

Flirty Feathers 100

Swirled Flirty Feather 100

Filled Flirty Feather 101

Square and Straight-Line Feathers 102

Parallel Single Feather 102

Parallel Single-Feather Corner 103

Square Spine Feather 105

Diagonal Feather 106

Radiating Diagonal Feather 108

Horizontal Feather 110

Border Block Feather 112

Half-Border Block Feather 115

Setting Triangles or Flying Geese Feathers 118

Curved Triangle 118

Curved Triangle Variation 121

Geometric Feather 123

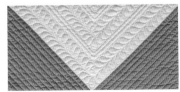

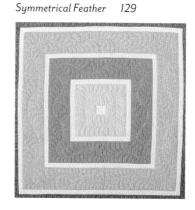
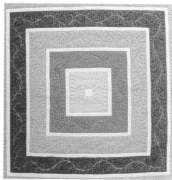
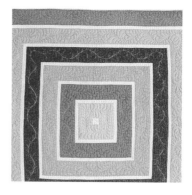

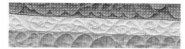
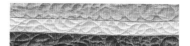

INTRODUCTION

I love to machine quilt feathers. I really, really love to machine quilt feathers. Yet after owning my longarm machine for about two years, I still had never even attempted to machine quilt a feather. I often would tell my mom, Kathleen, that I didn't think I'd ever machine quilt a feather— I didn't think I would ever have a quilt that feathers would be appropriate on. Was I naive!

The day finally arrived—I had a quilt that I knew needed feathers. I drew every single feather on the border of the quilt. It took forever to draw those feathers, and when I was done with the quilting, the result was stunning. Ever since that day, I think I've tried to include feathers on almost every single quilt I've quilted. Did I mention that I really love feathers?

I think there is a time and place for different feather styles. I love the look of traditional heirloom feathers, but I don't think they are appropriate for every single quilt.

There are traditional feathers and there are more modern, playful feathers—and when they are used on the right quilt, they make it shine.

In this book there are more than 60 different feather ideas, including block and border designs. I hope that you will come to love feathers as much as I do.

What makes a feather
MODERN?

Feathers are not new; they may be the most common, most recognized quilting motif. Traditionally feathers were hand quilted, and the women and men who quilted them often used stencils to get a precise design. Feathers and fancy motifs were a way to show off skills and make quilts dazzle. Feathers are often quilted using trapunto, a technique of putting two layers of batting behind the feather to make the feather pop on the quilt.

So what makes a feather "modern"? Traditional or heirloom feathers are very precise and perfect. The feathers are exactly the same size, and the spine is most often measured out and marked. I love traditional feathers and have a great appreciation for them. In this book, however, I'm sharing my ideas on breaking away from tradition—being creative with your feathers and letting go of perfection.

In this book I share three basic techniques for quilting feathers: *single feathers* (page 10), *bump back feathers* (page 11), and *curl feathers* (page 12). I recommend starting with the single-feather technique and, after you have mastered that, moving on to the bump back feathers and then the curl feathers. With the single feathers, you do not need to go back exactly along your original stitch line; when you quilt bump back feathers, however, you do need to stitch over the top of the feather, and this pattern looks much better if you stitch *exactly* over your original stitch line. For either type of feather, I always begin by stitching the spine. From there you will move on to stitching the feather. Most of the designs in this book can be achieved by stitching your feather with either process.

SINGLE FEATHER

Some examples of single feathers are the Feathered Center Diamond (page 23), Curved Center Feather (page 31), Paired Center Pod Feather (page 38), Matchstick Pod Feather (page 50), and Simple Binary Feather (page 61).

1. Stitch a single spine. I generally start at the bottom of the feather and stitch to the top. *figure A*

2. At this point you can either stitch back down the spine or cut your threads and start again at the bottom of the spine. Starting from the bottom point of the spine, stitch a single feather on the right side. *figure B*

3. Stitch a second feather on the top of the first feather, stitching in the same manner; there can be a small space between the first and second feather. *figure C*

4. Stitch a third feather in the same manner as the first 2 feathers, and repeat this pattern until all the feathers on the right side of the spine are complete. *figure D*

5. Stitch the feathers on the left side of the spine in the same manner.

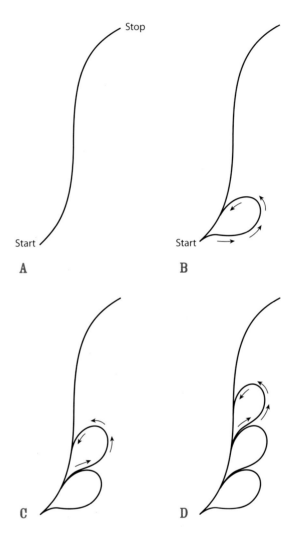

BUMP BACK FEATHER

Some examples of the bump back feather are the Figure-Eight Pod Feather (page 48), Mirrored Binary Feather (page 67), Capsule Feather (page 71), and Propeller Feather (page 80).

1. Stitch a single spine. I generally start at the bottom of the feather and stitch to the top. *figure A*

2. Starting from the bottom point of the spine, stitch a single feather on the bottom right side. *figure B*

3. To stitch a second feather, come from the spine and then stitch over the top and to the bottom feather. *figure C*

4. Stitch up around the outside of the feather and then stitch a third feather coming from the outside to the inside. *figure D*

5. Repeat Steps 3 and 4, stitching a bump back feather on every other feather.

6. Stitch the second side in exactly the same manner as the right side.

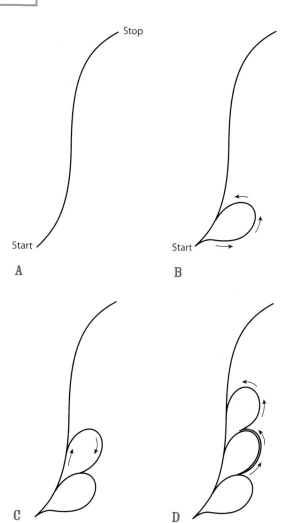

CURL FEATHER

Some examples of the Curl Feather are Curl Pod Feather with Ribbon Candy Fill (page 44), Hook Feather (page 66), Seedling Feather (page 86), and Sunflower Medallion Feather (page 94).

1. Stitch a single spine. I generally start at the bottom of the feather and stitch to the top. At this point you can either stitch back down the spine or cut the threads and start again at the bottom of the spine. *figure A*

2. At this point you can either stitch back down the spine or cut your threads and start again at the bottom of the spine. Starting from the bottom point of the spine, stitch a single curl feather on the right side; you'll stitch to the inside of the curl and then all the way back out along the same line. If you veer off the original line a little bit, it gives the feather a more casual and modern look. *figure B*

3. Stitch a second curl feather on the top of the first one, stitching in the same manner; there can be a small space between the first and second feather. *figure C*

4. Stitch a third curl feather in the same manner as the first two feathers, and repeat this pattern until all the feathers on the right side of the spine are complete.

5. Stitch the feathers on the left side of the spine in the same manner. *figure D*

tip ◆ When machine quilting feathers, you often need to join segments of feathers together, especially when quilting a medallion or a border—it can become tricky to fit feathers together. This is what I love about modern feathers: they don't all have to be the same size. Let go of perfection. You'll enjoy these feathers so much more.

If you're having a hard time fitting in the feathers and gauging spacing, I recommend using a blue water-soluble marker and marking the feathers. When you're about 3˝ from the feather or edge you will be meeting, draw the feathers in to fill in the space before you stitch them. Although you are drawing them first, you can erase or re-draw as needed. This will help you learn to gauge the spacing—and also give you practice getting nice feather shapes.

BASICS

Machine quilting feathers can be daunting. Traditionally we are taught that feathers have to be perfect and must be very uniform. I like to turn this around by thinking of feathers as being flirty or playful. There's no reason why you can't break the traditional rules (while still respecting them), let go of any fears, and have fun with feathers.

In this book you'll see, step by step, how to machine quilt a variety of feather patterns that fit every kind of space on your quilt.

The following section briefly covers tools and basic quiltmaking techniques so that you can move on to the fun stuff, machine quilting feathers. If you want more information on the basics or are looking for additional quilting patterns, I recommend my books Beginner's Guide to Free-Motion Quilting *and* Next Steps in Machine Quilting *(both available from Stash Books).*

MARKING

Even if you are an experienced quilter, it will be helpful to mark a few guidelines on your quilt before you start stitching. I like to use a blue Mark-B-Gone water-soluble marker.

To remove the marks, use a squirt bottle with plain water to spritz away the marking ink. In some cases the ink may have migrated from the quilt top into the batting fibers. If this has happened, saturate the marks and blot with an absorbent paper towel or cloth.

Important: *Do not leave the quilt in sunlight or near a heat source or iron the quilt until you are sure all the markings are fully removed.*

SEWING MACHINE

Free-motion machine quilting can be done successfully on most conventional home sewing machines, as long as the machine has a free-motion foot (see Machine Feet, next page) and the ability to drop the feed-dogs (the little teeth that move the fabric from underneath). I currently have a BERNINA Aurora 450. It is most helpful if your machine is set into a sewing table, creating a large working area that can make it easier to maneuver your quilt under the needle.

MACHINE FEET

A free-motion foot is essential. They come in assorted shapes and may be plastic or metal. They are called by different names, including *darning* or *hopping foot*. A foot with a clear plastic sole is great because it provides improved visibility.

NEEDLES

Three types of needles are recommended for machine quilting on a home sewing machine: quilting needles, embroidery needles, and topstitch needles. Each has advantages. Quilting needles have a slim, tapered point and a slightly stronger shaft for stitching through fabric layers and across intersecting seams. Machine quilting can also be done using topstitch needles, which have an extra-sharp point and a larger eye and can accommodate heavier threads. Embroidery needles are similar to "universal" needles, but they have a larger eye.

I prefer to use a titanium-coated topstitch needle. Titanium-coated needles last up to five times longer than regular needles. I recommend the needles made by Superior Threads, but you may choose among the many others that are available.

It is very important that your needle is the correct size for the thread you are using. I recommend three sizes for quilting: 80/12 for machine quilting with fine thread, 90/14 for machine quilting with medium-weight thread, and 100/16 for machine quilting with heavy-weight thread.

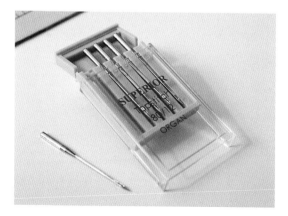

THREAD

Choosing the correct thread for machine quilting can seem overwhelming. The most common types of thread are cotton, polyester, and polyester-wrapped cotton thread.

I prefer to always use a lightweight thread (such as So Fine! by Superior Threads for the top and Bottom Line by Superior Threads for the bobbin), but you can certainly try various threads and brands to determine what look you prefer. A thicker thread will show up more on your quilt, while a thinner thread will blend into the fabric a bit more.

As for choosing thread color, I recommend using the same color thread on the top and bottom. As you gain more confidence in your machine quilting, you can change the top and bottom thread colors, but most often matching threads ensure better results.

I love the convenience of prewound bobbins; they save time, they are easy to use, they are available from most thread companies in several colors, and they are always wound perfectly.

> *tip* ◆ If you really want your machine quilting to pop, create a faux trapunto look by using a slightly off-colored thread. For example, on white fabric, use off-white thread. This will give your quilt the appearance of extra texture without the extra work.

THREAD TENSION

Good thread tension means that the stitching looks good on both sides of the quilt, with an equal amount of thread on the top and bottom and no loops. Loopy threads mean that your tension is too loose; puckered and pulled threads mean it is too tight.

Adjusting tension can be tricky, because you may have to adjust both the top *and* the bobbin tension. Most newer machines have a recommended tension setting, which for free-motion quilting is often lower than for piecing. Top tension is very easy to adjust using the machine's tension gauge. It is often the bottom tension, however, that can make all the difference. Adjusting the bobbin tension can be done by turning the screw on the bobbin case just a small amount. Turn left to loosen the tension and right to tighten it. You may need to refer to your machine's owners' manual, especially if your machine has a drop-in bobbin case rather than a removable one.

I recommend checking tension before you begin machine quilting and after each bobbin fill.

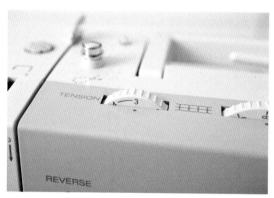

Top tension gauge

Adjusting tension screw on bobbin case

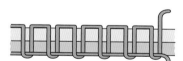

Top tension too loose or bottom tension too tight

Top tension too tight or bottom tension too loose

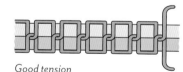

Good tension

BATTING

Batting is the filling between the quilt top and backing in the quilt sandwich. Batting affects the look and feel of the quilt. The importance of batting is often overlooked.

When choosing batting, you need to first determine the look that you want to achieve. Do you want a very flat quilt with little texture, or do you want to create more texture and make your machine quilting really pop? Neither look is right or wrong; it just depends on what you want.

Always make sure that you check the batting manufacturer's recommended quilting density; this can vary from 2˝–4˝ between stitch lines to up to 8˝ between stitch lines.

For machine quilting on a domestic machine, the most commonly used battings are poly/cotton blends, which generally are slightly loftier than 100% cotton and a little more breathable than 100% polyester. The most common brands are the Hobbs 80/20 blend, Quilters Dream 70/30 blend, and Warm and Natural 80/20 blend. I have used all of these, and all work fine; I prefer the look and feel of the Quilters Dream 70/30 blend.

Quilters Dream Poly Deluxe is another favorite batting of mine. I love the dimension this batting creates, yet when it is washed, it's very drapable. It's also a lower-loft batting than most polyester battings.

If you want more texture, however, try using more than one layer of batting. Occasionally when I machine quilt, I use a layer of Quilters Dream Poly Deluxe on the bottom and a layer of Quilters Dream Wool on the top.

tip ◆ If you're going to use two layers of batting, use the wool or loftier batting on the top and the denser batting on the bottom. This makes the batting puff toward the top of the quilt.

LAYERING AND BASTING

To prepare for layering and basting, cut the backing and batting 4˝ larger than the quilt top on all sides. Make sure that the quilt top is squared up, the top and backing are pressed, and all threads are clipped.

You will need a large, flat surface, such as a table, clean floor, or carpet. Place the quilt backing wrong side up on the table or floor. Tape it down with masking tape or use clamps to hold the backing flat on a table. If you are on a carpet, use T-pins to pin it flat.

Center and place the batting flat on the backing, and then center the quilt top right side up on the top of the batting. Now you can begin to baste.

Basting can be done using spray baste, basting thread, or safety pins. No matter which method you choose, it is very important that the layers are completely flat and positioned

correctly. It's important to take the time to baste properly, as this will help ensure better results when machine quilting your quilt. I recommend trying all three methods to find which suits you best.

Spray basting can be great, because there are no pins for you to stop and take out and no thread to worry about getting caught in your machine foot. It can, however, be very messy, and generally you need to spray baste outside. Follow the instructions on the can to spray baste between each layer.

With **thread basting**, occasionally thread can get caught in the hopping foot of your machine and cause you to get out of your groove while free-motion quilting. On the plus side, thread basting is very easy to remove, and it is not messy like spray. When basting with thread by hand or machine,

stitch a line horizontally, then vertically, and then diagonally across the quilt, using stitches much longer than normal to create a single line each way. Then begin to fill in, making a grid across the quilt with stitched lines about 6˝ apart to evenly secure the quilt layers.

Pin basting has the advantage of reusable pins, but if you're in your groove and have to stop to remove a pin, it can be very annoying. For pin basting use size 1 or 2 safety pins. Curved quilting pins work especially well. I recommend using approximately 75 pins for a crib-size quilt and up to 350 pins for a queen-size quilt. Start pinning at the center of the quilt, making sure to pin all three layers together and spacing the pins about a palm width apart. Pin outward horizontally and vertically, creating a gridlike pattern.

STITCHING DIRECTION

As you begin to stitch feathers, you may discover that you have preferences as to which side of the feather spine you prefer to start on and in which direction you prefer to stitch—right to left or left to right. Go with whatever is most comfortable for you. After you understand the basic structure of each feather design, you should stitch it in the way that works best for you.

I am right handed, and it feels more comfortable to stitch the right side of a feather first, then the left. Some people start with the left side, and some people actually find it easier to move back and forth from one side to the other.

NOTE

Many of the feather patterns in this book have been stitched on half-square triangle blocks, Flying Geese, or other pieced shapes. Some are shown on plain blocks. Regardless of how the quilting is shown, most of the quilting patterns will work on any type of block, pieced or plain, and even blocks that aren't square—simply adjust your quilting to fit your space. That said, there are a few patterns that are specifically designed for triangular shapes such as Flying Geese, and these will be noted.

Quilting
DESIGNS

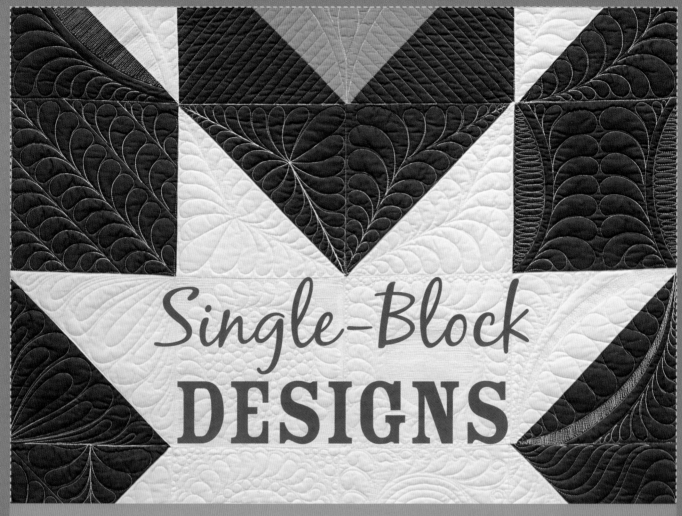

Single-Block DESIGNS

DIAMOND FEATHERS

Feathered Center Diamond

The Feathered Center Diamond is a fun, playful design that works for many different types of quilts.

tip ◆ My favorite curved rulers for machine quilting and marking are the curved templates available at The Quilted Pineapple (thequiltedpineapple.com). I have the complete set because they are so useful for so many block sizes.

STEP 1 Use a water-soluble marker to mark the center point on all four sides of the block. Use those marks to draw straight lines horizontally and vertically through the center of the block. Then mark curved lines from center point to center point.

STEP 2 Start quilting at the bottom of the block. Stitch along the curved lines from point to point.

STEP 3 Start stitching feathers at the bottom on the left side of the curved line. Continue stitching the outside feathers around the entire block.

STEP 4 After you have stitched the feathers around the outside of the whole block, move to the center. Begin at the bottom of the block and fill in to the centerlines drawn in Step 1.

STEP 5 Repeat feathers around the inside of the entire block.

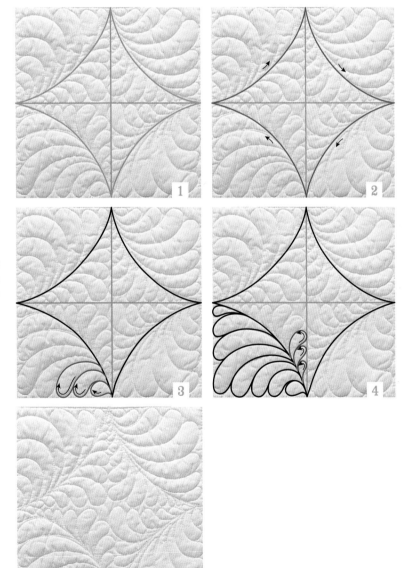

Hatched Center Diamond Feather

The Hatched Center Diamond design is a traditional design, but its curved crosshatching in the center gives it more of a modern flair.

STEP 1 *Use a water-soluble marker to mark the center point on all 4 sides of the block. Use those marks to draw curved lines from center point to center point.*

STEP 2 *Start quilting at the bottom of the block and stitch along the curved lines from point to point.*

STEP 3 *After you have stitched the curved lines all the way around the block, begin stitching feathers at the bottom left.*

STEP 4 *Stitch the remaining feathers around the block, moving clockwise.*

STEP 5 *After you have stitched feathers around the whole block, stitch about ½˝ up from the original curved stitch line. Next stitch an echoed curved line from the bottom left to the right side of the curve. Travel along the original curved stitch line and move up about ½˝. Then stitch a second curved line.*

STEP 6 *Repeat stitching curved lines back and forth and traveling along the original curved line until you fill the block completely.*

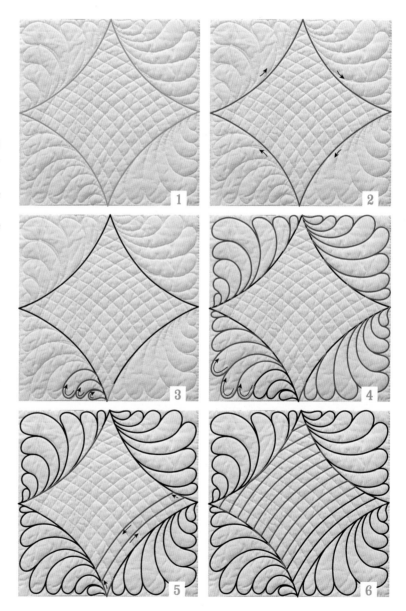

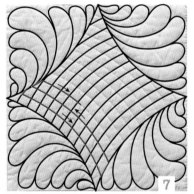

STEP 7 *After you have stitched all those lines, travel in the original curved stitch line and move to the top left corner of the diamond. From this point begin stitching curved lines, traveling about ½″ along the original stitch line to fill in the curved lines perpendicular to the lines in Step 6.*

Square-in-a-Square Diamond Feather

This fun Square-in-a-Square Diamond Feather has a modern feel when quilted in a plain quilt block, yet it can play nicely with a more traditional pieced block as well.

STEP 1 *Use a water-soluble marker to mark the center point on all four sides of the block. Draw straight lines from marked point to marked point. Then move in about ½˝ and mark another set of straight lines inside the previous lines. If you're using this design on a small block, you may want to draw your lines a bit closer together; the block shown here is 10˝ × 10˝. Finally, draw straight lines horizontally and vertically through the center of the block.*

STEP 2 *Begin stitching at the bottom point of the first drawn line. Stitch around all 4 sides, following the lines and ending back at the bottom point.*

STEP 3 *Stitch the first feather on the outside of the straight line at the bottom left.*

STEP 4 *Continue stitching feathers around the outside of the entire block. Stop and cut the threads.*

STEP 5 *Stitch along the inner straight lines, and then start stitching feathers on the inner straight line.*

STEP 6 *Continue stitching feathers all the way around the inside of the block, using the drawn lines as your reference for where to stop the feathers.*

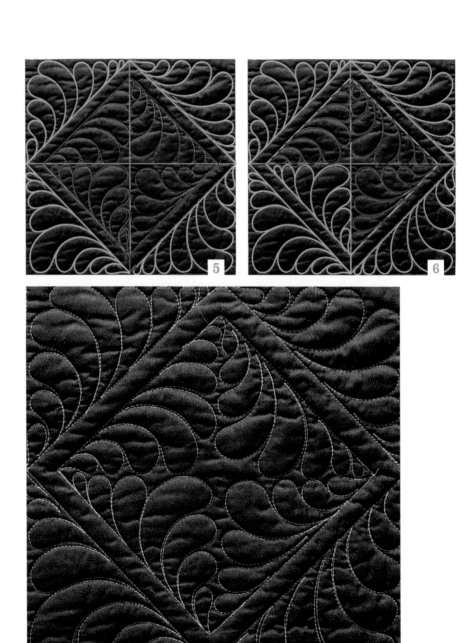

Straight-Lined Center Diamond

The straight lines in the center of this block give it a light, open feel. If you want to quilt this design on a solid block, draw a diagonal line from the lower left corner to the upper right corner.

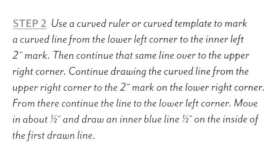

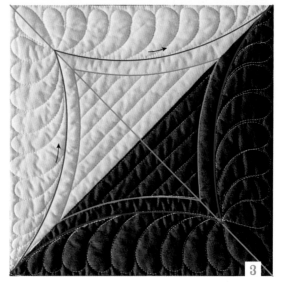

STEP 1 Use a water-soluble marker to draw a straight line diagonally through the center of the block, from the upper left corner to the lower right corner. Then mark a little line 2˝ from the corner of the block on both sides, and then a second line about ½˝ in from the 2˝ mark. If you're using this design on a small block, you may want to draw your little lines a bit closer to the corners of the block; the block shown here is 10˝ square.

STEP 2 Use a curved ruler or curved template to mark a curved line from the lower left corner to the inner left 2˝ mark. Then continue that same line over to the upper right corner. Continue drawing the curved line from the upper right corner to the 2˝ mark on the lower right corner. From there continue the line to the lower left corner. Move in about ½˝ and draw an inner blue line ½˝ on the inside of the first drawn line.

STEP 3 Begin stitching in the upper left corner and follow the drawn outer curved line around the block back to the starting point.

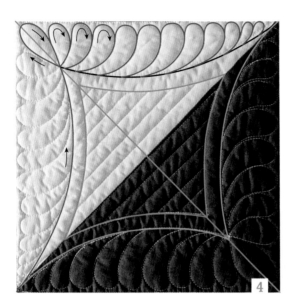

STEP 4 *From the upper left corner, begin stitching feathers out to the upper right corner.*

STEP 5 *When you get to the upper right corner, follow your curved line back to the upper left corner. From there stitch feathers back down along the curve to the bottom left corner.*

STEP 6 *Travel along the curved line to the lower right corner. Repeat Steps 4 and 5 to quilt the feathers on the right side of the block. Stop stitching.*

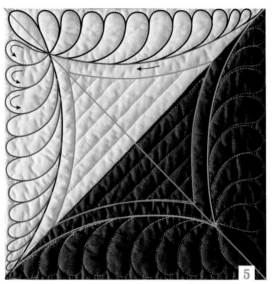

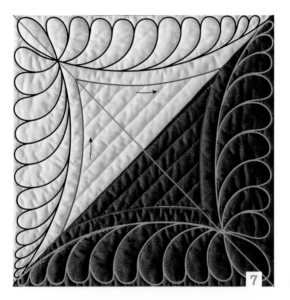
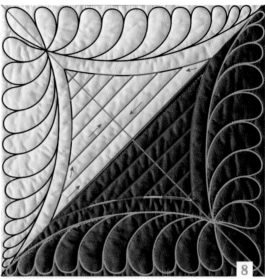

STEP 7 *Begin stitching at the bottom right corner of the inner curved line and stitch the curved line all the way around the inside of the block.*

STEP 8 *From the lower right corner, stitch the straight lines, traveling along the curved line, to fill in the center of the block.*

STRETCHED CENTERS

Curved Center Feather

With the Curved Center Feather design, if you use a thread color that blends nicely with your fabrics, it will create a beautiful secondary pattern. The block shown here is quilted in contrasting thread to highlight the pattern.

STEP 1 Use a curved ruler or template and a water-soluble marker to mark curved lines from each of the corners. Then mark an X through the center of the block.

STEP 2 Stitch all the way around the block, beginning in the lower left corner.

STEP 3 Begin stitching feathers around the outside of the curved line, starting in the lower left corner and continuing around the block.

STEP 4 After you have stitched feathers around the outside of the entire block, move to the inside and fill in with feathers. Use the blue marked line as a reference for how big to make the feathers.

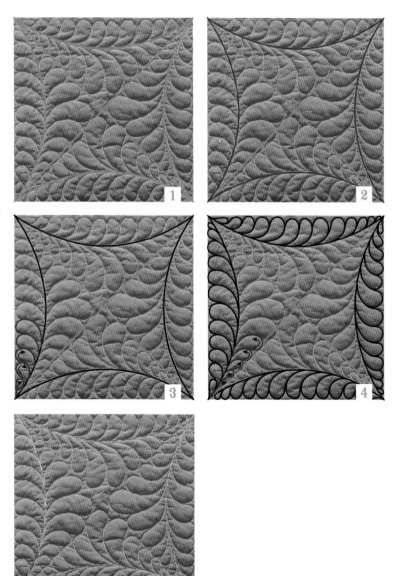

Curved Center Feather with Pebbles

The Curved Center Feather with Pebbles is a fun, more modern play on the Curved Center Feather (page 31). In this design quilted pebbles fill in the outer curve, but you can easily fill in with your favorite filler to add a more modern flair.

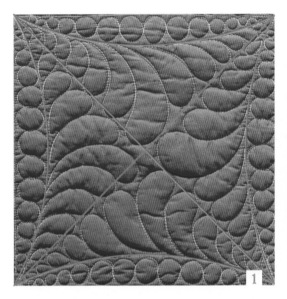

STEP 1 *Use a curved ruler or template and a water-soluble marker to mark curved lines from each of the corners. Then mark an X through the center of the block.*

STEP 2 *Stitch all the way around the block, beginning in the lower left corner.*

STEP 3 *Begin stitching feathers, filling in the inside of the block. Use the drawn X as a reference for how big to make the feathers.*

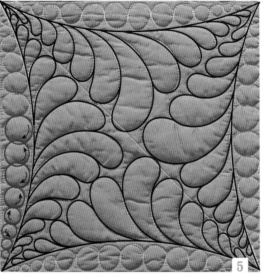

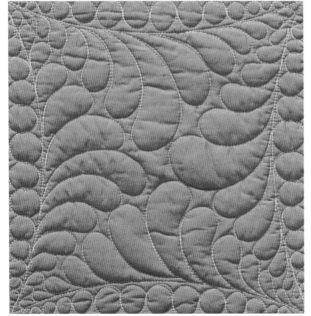

STEP 4 *Fill in the inside of the block completely with feathers.*

STEP 5 *After all feathers are quilted, move to the outside of the curved line. Begin filling in circles on the outside of the line, stitching in an over-under method—stitch over the top of the circle, then around the bottom, and then back over the top.*

Arrow Center Feather

This Arrow Center design is great for half-square triangles, Hour Glass, or even solid quilt blocks. The straight-line quilting adds a decidedly modern look.

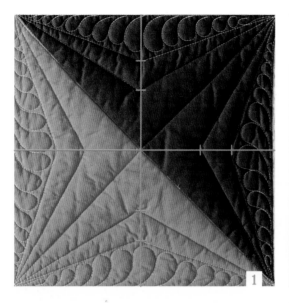

STEP 1 *Use a water-soluble marker to mark the center point on all four sides of the block. Use those marks to draw straight lines horizontally and vertically through the center of the block. Then, on all four sides, draw a small mark 1½˝ from the center of the block on the horizontal and vertical lines. Draw a second mark about ½˝ farther out from that.*

tip ◆ If the block is smaller or larger, you may want to space your marks a bit differently and use fewer or more straight lines to fill in appropriately.

STEP 2 *Stitch an X through the center of the block starting at the lower left corner and stitching up to the upper right corner. Then stitch-in-the-ditch down to the lower right corner and back up through the center of the block to the upper left corner.*

STEP 3 *Stitch from the upper left corner to the inner point on the left side of the block. Continue stitching from corner to inner point and then back out to the corner around the entire block.*

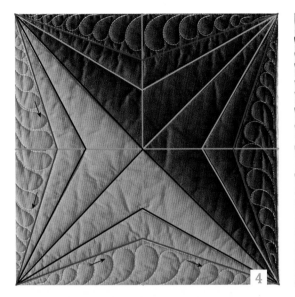

STEP 4 *Stitch from the upper left corner to the outer point on the left side of the block. Continue stitching from corner to outer point and then back out to the corner around the entire block.*

STEP 5 *From the upper left corner, begin stitching feathers, filling in all the way around the outside of the block with feathers.*

Double-Dip Feather

The Double-Dip Feather is fun as a single-block design, but you can quilt them in multiple blocks, in a row, or on top of each other to create a simple yet stunning secondary pattern.

STEP 1 *Use a water-soluble marker and a curved ruler or template to mark a curved line from the upper left corner to the lower left corner. Mark a mirror-image curve on the right side. Move over about ½˝ and mark a second curve on both sides of the block. Then draw a straight vertical line through the center of the block.*

STEP 2 *Start stitching in the upper left corner and follow the outer curved line to the bottom left corner.*

STEP 3 *From the lower left corner, stitch loops, filling in the curve completely to the upper left corner.*

STEP 4 *Stitch-in-the-ditch over to the second curved line, and then stitch down that line to the bottom of the block.*

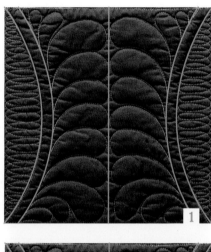

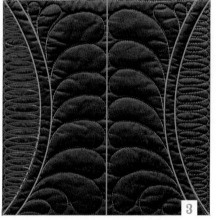

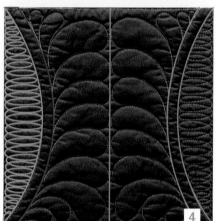

STEP 5 *From the bottom of the block, stitch feathers up the curve, using the center drawn line as a reference to quilt to.*

STEP 6 *Stitch-in-the-ditch along the top edge of the block to the top right corner. From there use the same pattern that you used on the left side of the block to fill in the right side of the block.*

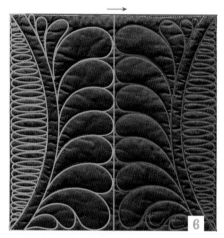

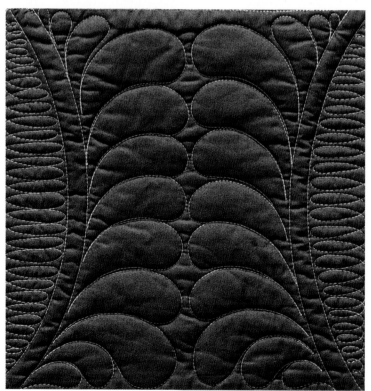

POD FEATHERS

Paired Center Pod Feather

This fun Paired Center Pod Feather design is a twist on modern and traditional. The heavy quilting in the center of the design adds contrast and makes the feathers pop.

STEP 1 *Use a water-soluble marker and a curved ruler or template to mark a curved line from the lower left corner of the block to the upper right corner of the block. Move in about ½˝ and mark a second pair of curved lines.*

STEP 2 *Begin stitching on the upper right corner and stitch down to the lower left corner.*

STEP 3 *From the lower left corner, stitch feathers up the left side of the block to the upper right corner.*

STEP 4 *From the upper right corner, stitch along the outer curved line back to the lower left corner. From there stitch feathers up the outer right side of the curved line.*

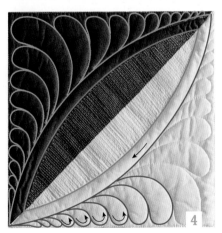

STEP 5 *From the upper right corner, stitch-in-the-ditch down ½˝ to the inner curved line. Stitch along that line from the upper right down to the bottom left and then back up to the upper right.*

STEP 6 *Stitch back and forth with closely spaced straight lines to completely fill in the center of the pod.*

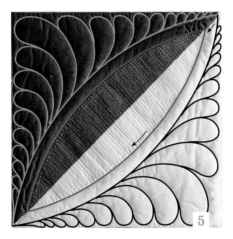

Spinning Pod Feather

The Spinning Pod Feather is a fun and playful design because the pattern of the quilting gives the block a sense of rotation.

STEP 1 *Use a water-soluble marker and a curved ruler or template to draw a curved line from the lower left corner to the upper right corner. Draw a second line from the upper right corner back down to the lower left corner. Then draw a second curved line from the lower left corner to about ½˝ away from the upper right corner, and a third curved line from the lower left corner to about 1˝ from the upper right corner. Repeat this pattern from the upper right corner to the lower left corner.*

STEP 2 *Stitch from the lower left corner to the upper right corner along the curved drawn line. Stitch from the upper right back down to the lower left on the curved drawn line.*

STEP 3 *Stitch from the lower left corner along the second left curved line up to the upper right. Stitch-in-the-ditch over to the third line, and stitch back down to the lower left corner.*

STEP 4 *On the outside of the third stitch line, fill in the open space with feathers.*

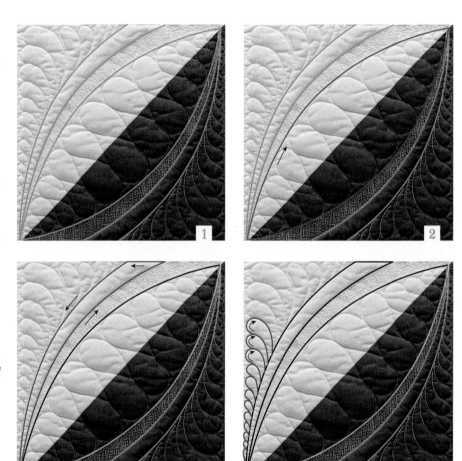

STEP 5 *Stitch-in-the-ditch to the upper right corner. Fill in with tight, straight lines between the first and second curved lines, filling in down to the lower left corner.*

STEP 6 *Stitch a Ribbon Candy pattern from the lower left corner to the upper right corner of the pod, filling it completely.*

STEP 7 *Repeating the previous steps, fill in the right side of the pod in the same pattern that was quilted on the left side of the pod.*

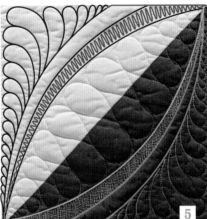

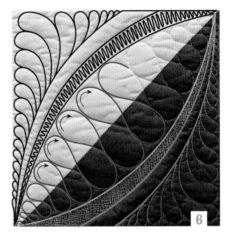

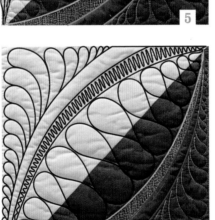

Simple Pod Feather

The Simple Pod Feather is simple yet elegant.

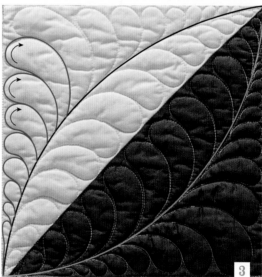

STEP 1 *Use a water-soluble marker and a curved ruler or template to mark a curved line from the lower left corner to the upper right corner and then back to the lower left corner. If you want to quilt this design on a solid block, draw a diagonal line from the lower left corner to the upper right corner.*

STEP 2 *Stitch from the lower left corner to the upper right corner along the curved line, and then stitch back down to the lower left corner.*

STEP 3 *Stitch feathers from the lower left corner up the outside of the curved line, filling in the outside of the curve.*

STEP 4 *Stitch-in-the-ditch from the upper right corner to the lower left corner. From the lower left corner, completely fill in the inside of the curve with feathers.*

STEP 5 *From the upper right corner stitch-in-the-ditch down to the lower right corner and then along the bottom to the lower left corner. Stitch feathers along the outside of the right side, down the center of the block again, and then up the inner right side of the pod.*

Curl Pod Feather

The Curl Pod Feather is a fun way to dress up the Simple Pod Feather (page 42). This fun design is shown on a half-square triangle but would also be beautiful quilted on a solid-colored block.

STEP 1 *Use a water-soluble marker and a curved ruler or template to mark a curved line from the lower left corner to the upper right corner. Then mark the opposite side from the upper right corner to the lower left corner. If you want to quilt this design on a solid block, draw a diagonal line from the lower left corner to the upper right corner.*

STEP 2 *Starting in the lower left corner, stitch up the curved line to the upper right corner and then down the other curved line.*

STEP 3 *Begin stitching regular feathers alternating with curl feathers in the lower left corner along the curved line.*

STEP 4 *Continue to alternate stitching feathers and curl feathers, following the curved line up to the right corner. When you get to the top, stitch-in-the-ditch to get from the upper right corner to the lower left corner.*

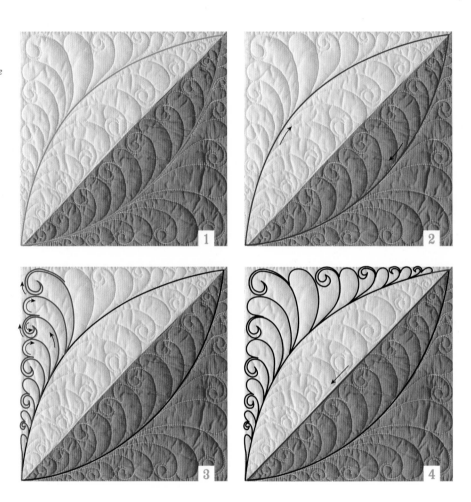

STEP 5 *Stitch feathers, filling in the inside of the curve and repeating the same pattern as on the outside of the curve, alternating feather and curl feather.*

STEP 6 *Stitch-in-the-ditch to get from the upper right corner to the lower right corner and then along the bottom back to the lower left corner.*

STEP 7 *Repeat the process on the right side of the curve: stitch to fill in the outside, stitch-in-the-ditch, and then fill in the inside of the curve.*

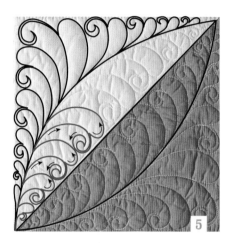

Curl Pod Feather with Ribbon Candy Fill

The Curl Pod Feather with Ribbon Candy Fill is a fun play on the Curl Pod Feather (page 44).

STEP 1 *Use a water-soluble marker and a curved ruler or template to mark a curved line from the lower left corner to the upper right corner and from the upper right corner to the lower left corner.*

STEP 2 *Starting in the lower left corner, stitch along the curved line from the lower left corner to the upper right corner and then from the upper right corner back down to the lower right corner.*

STEP 3 *From the lower left corner, alternate stitching feathers and curl feathers, filling in the left side of the curve.*

STEP 4 *From the upper right corner, stitch-in-the-ditch down to the lower right corner and then along the bottom side to the lower left corner.*

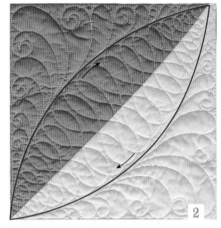

STEP 5 *Fill in the alternating feathers and curls along the right side of the curved line.*

STEP 6 *Stitch from the upper right corner, filling in the center of the pod with a crossover Ribbon Candy pattern.*

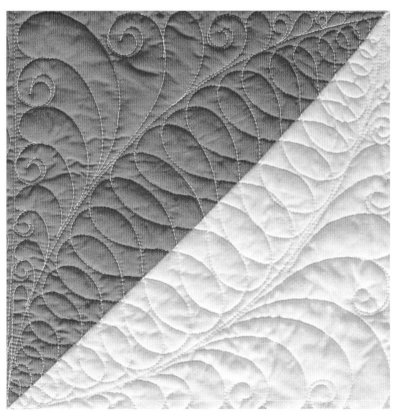

Figure-Eight Pod Feather

The Figure-Eight Pod Feather is a fun, simple twist on the Simple Pod Feather (page 42).

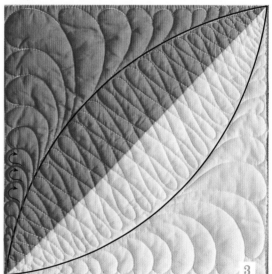

STEP 1 *Use a water-soluble marker and a curved ruler or template or plate to mark a curved line from the lower left corner to the upper right corner, and then from the upper right corner to the lower left corner.*

STEP 2 *Starting in the lower left corner, stitch along the curved line up to the upper right corner and then from the upper right corner back down to the lower left corner.*

STEP 3 *Stitch feathers on the left side of the curved line.*

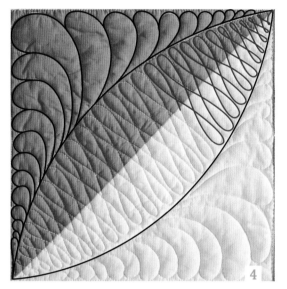

STEP 4 *From the upper right corner, fill in the center of the pod shape with a figure-eight pattern.*

STEP 5 *From the bottom left corner, stitch feathers on the right side of the curved line.*

Matchstick Pod Feather

The Matchstick Pod Feather is an elegant design with the matchstick background quilting putting the graceful feathers in the foreground.

 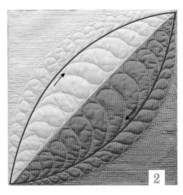 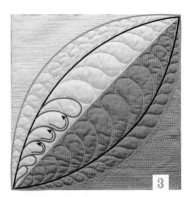

STEP 1 *Use a water-soluble marker and a curved ruler or template to mark a curved line from the lower left corner to the upper right corner. Use a slightly different-shaped curve to draw a line slightly outside of the first curved line. If you want to quilt this design on a solid block, draw a diagonal line from the lower left corner to the upper right corner.*

STEP 2 *Begin stitching in the lower left corner. Stitch along the inner curved line, from the lower left corner to the upper right corner. From the upper right corner, stitch back to the lower left corner.*

STEP 3 *From the lower left corner, stitch feathers along the inner left curve, filling in to the centerline.*

STEP 4 *From the upper right corner, stitch along the outer right curved line back to the lower left corner.*

STEP 5 *Stitch feathers from the lower left corner, filling in the inside of the inner right curve.*

STEP 6 *From the upper right corner, stitch along the upper curved line back down to the lower left corner. From there begin filling in feathers in the outer left curve.*

STEP 7 *From the upper right corner, stitch back-and-forth horizontal straight lines, filling in the outside left side of the feather.*

STEP 8 *From the lower left corner, fill in the feathers on the right side of the curve.*

STEP 9 *From the upper right corner, stitch back-and-forth horizontal straight lines, filling in the outside right side of the feather.*

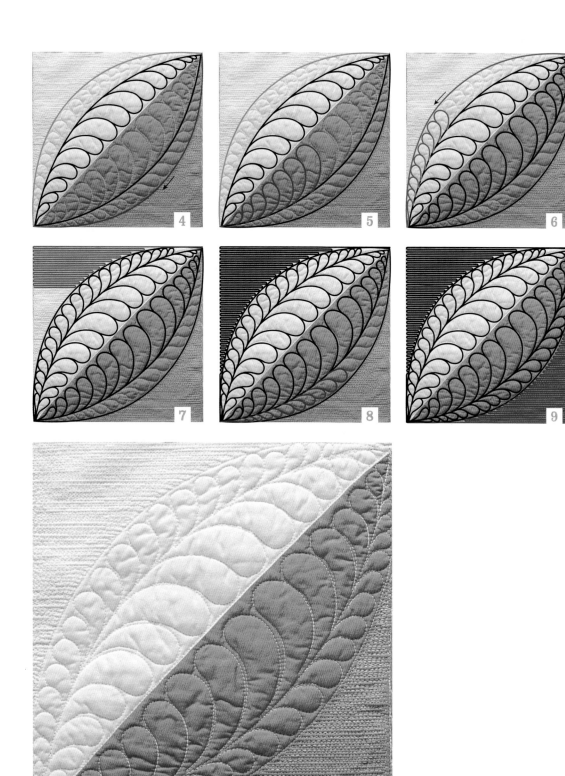

Diamond Pod Feather

The Diamond Pod Feather has a simple point in the center, adding just a bit of crispness to a traditional feather.

STEP 1 *Use a water-soluble marker to draw a line from the upper left corner to the lower right corner. Measure about 2˝ from the centerline and make a small mark on both sides. If you want to quilt this design on a solid block, draw a diagonal line from the lower left corner to upper right corner. If you're using this design on a small block, you may want to draw your marks a bit closer to the centerline; the block shown here is 10˝ square.*

STEP 2 *From the lower left corner, stitch a straight line to the left-side 2˝ mark. From there stitch to the upper right corner. From the upper right corner, stitch a straight line to the right-side 2˝ mark and then stitch back to the lower left corner.*

STEP 3 *From the lower left corner, stitch feathers, filling in the inside of the left half of the diamond shape.*

STEP 4 *From the upper right corner, stitch-in-the-ditch to the upper left corner and then to the lower left corner. Then stitch feathers along the top side of the spine.*

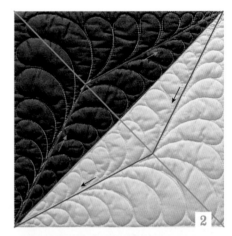

STEP 5 *From the upper right corner, stitch-in-the-ditch down the center of the block to the lower left corner.*

STEP 6 *From the lower left corner, stitch feathers along the inside of the right straight line.*

STEP 7 *Stitch-in-the-ditch from the upper right corner to the lower right corner and then along the bottom edge to the lower left corner. From there fill in the outer right side of the straight line with feathers.*

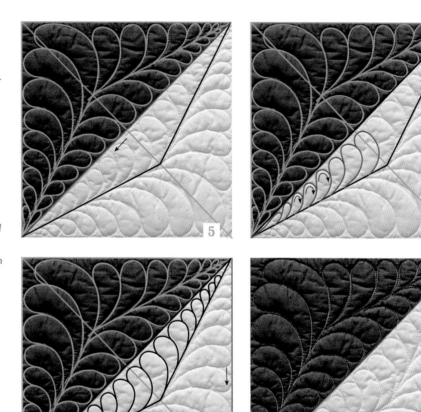

Centered Diamond Pod Feather

In the Centered Diamond Pod Feather, the feathers radiate from a central point on each side of the block.

STEP 1 *Use a water-soluble marker to draw a straight line from the upper left corner to the lower right corner. If you want to quilt this design on a solid block, draw a diagonal line from the lower left corner to upper right corner. Mark 2 dots, about 2˝ from the centerline. If you're using this design on a small block you may want to draw your marks a bit closer to the centerline; the block shown here is 10˝ square.*

STEP 2 *Begin stitching at the upper 2˝ point. From there stitch a single top feather and then fill in feathers along the top left side of the line.*

STEP 3 *From the lower left corner, stitch a straight line to the 2˝ point. Start stitching feathers, filling in the bottom left triangle shape.*

STEP 4 *From the lower left corner, stitch-in-the-ditch to the upper right corner. From the upper right corner, stitch a straight line to the 2˝ point on the left side. Then stitch feathers to fill in the top right triangle shape.*

STEP 5 *From the upper right corner, stitch back along the straight line to the 2˝ point. Stitch feathers along the lower side of the upper line to fill in the left side of the block completely.*

STEP 6 *From the upper right corner, stitch the same pattern on the bottom side of the block as was stitched on the top side of the block.*

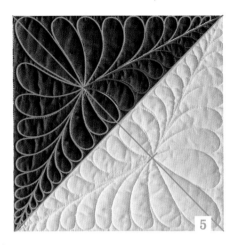

DOUBLE-CENTERED DIAMOND POD FEATHER VARIATION

The Double-Centered Diamond Pod Feather is an elegant variation of the Centered Diamond Pod Feather design.

When quilting this variation, simply stitch the second filler feather pattern as you stitch the first feather.

Point-to-Point Diamond Feather

The Point-to-Point Diamond Feather is a fun pattern that combines feathers with concentric center diamonds.

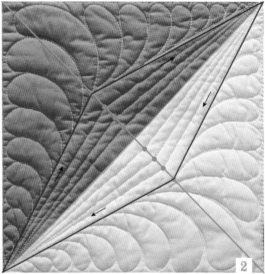

STEP 1 *Use a water-soluble marker to draw a straight line from the upper left corner to the lower right corner. If you want to quilt this design on a solid block, draw a diagonal line from the lower left corner to upper right corner. From the center point of the straight line, mark 4 dots ¼˝ apart on both sides of the straight line. If you are using a solid-colored block, draw in a diagonal line from the upper right to the lower left corner.*

STEP 2 *Stitch a straight line from the lower left corner to the outer dot on the straight line. Then stitch a straight line to the upper right corner. Repeat this same pattern on the right side of the block.*

STEP 3 *From the lower left corner, stitch feathers on the left side of the block, filling in the outside completely.*

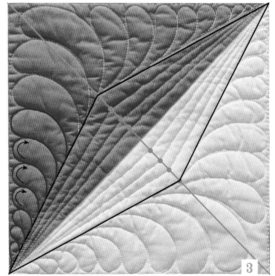

Point-to-Point Diamond Feather continued

STEP 4 *From the upper right corner, stitch a straight line to the first ¼˝ mark inside your original diamond and then back to the lower left corner. From there stitch feathers on the outer right side of the straight line, filling in to the top right corner.*

STEP 5 *From the upper right corner, stitch straight, point-to-point lines filling in the center of the diamond.*

Point-to-Point Feather Variation

The Point-to-Point Feather Variation is a simpler version of the Point-to-Point Diamond Feather (page 57). Use half of the design to quilt a setting triangle or Flying Geese triangle.

STEP 1 *Use a water-soluble marker to draw a straight line from the upper left corner to the lower right corner. If you want to quilt this design on a solid block, draw a diagonal line from the lower left corner to the upper right corner. From the center point, mark 2 dots ½˝ apart on each side of the line.*

STEP 2 *Stitch a straight line from the lower left corner to the left 1˝ mark. From there stitch a feather in to the top left corner and then fill in feathers down the left side of the block.*

STEP 3 *From the lower left corner, stitch a straight line to the inner ½˝ mark and then stitch to the upper right corner. From there stitch a straight line to the left 1˝ mark. Then stitch feathers along the top edge of the straight line.*

Point-to-Point Feather Variation continued

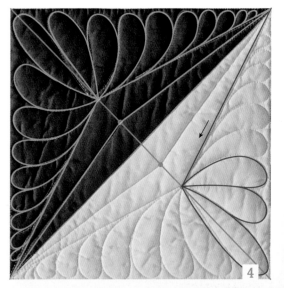

STEP 4 *From the upper right corner, stitch a straight line to the right 1˝ mark and then stitch feathers along the right side of that line.*

STEP 5 *Follow the same pattern stitched on the left side to fill in the feathers and straight lines on the right side of the block.*

BINARY FEATHERS

Simple Binary Feather

While the Simple Binary Feather is an uncomplicated design, it adds impact and stylish detail to any quilt. If you want to quilt this design on a solid block, draw a diagonal line from the lower left corner to the upper right corner.

STEP 1 *Beginning at the lower left corner, stitch feathers along the centerline, filling the left side of the block completely.*

STEP 2 *Stitch-in-the-ditch to get from the upper right corner back to the lower left corner. From there stitch feathers along the right side of the centerline.*

DETAILED BINARY FEATHER VARIATION

The Detailed Binary Feather is quilted in the same pattern as the Simple Binary Feather, but when you stitch every other feather of this design, add a simple straight line for just a bit of extra detail.

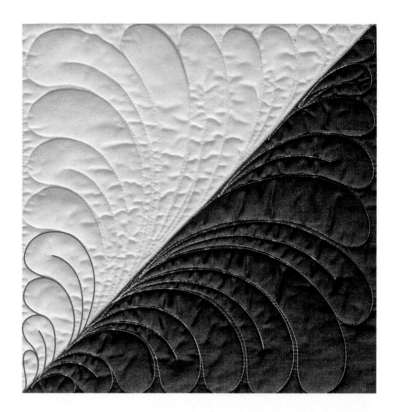

Rotating Binary Feather

The Rotating Binary Feather is a fun yet simple way to add a sense of motion to a quilt. If you want to quilt this design on a solid block, draw a diagonal line from the lower left corner to upper right corner.

STEP 1 *Starting in the upper right corner, stitch a straight line from the upper right corner to the lower left corner. Then stitch feathers up the right left side of the block.*

STEP 2 *From the upper right corner, stitch feathers down the right side of the straight line.*

Fern Feather

The Fern Feather is a variation on the traditional feather shape. This design is also beautiful quilted as a border. If you want to quilt this design on a solid block, draw a diagonal line from the lower left corner to upper right corner.

STEP 1 *Beginning in the lower left corner, stitch fern feathers filling in the left side of the block.*

STEP 2 *Stitch-in-the-ditch to get from the upper right corner back to the lower left corner.*

STEP 3 *Stitch fern feathers along the right side of the block, filling in the right side completely.*

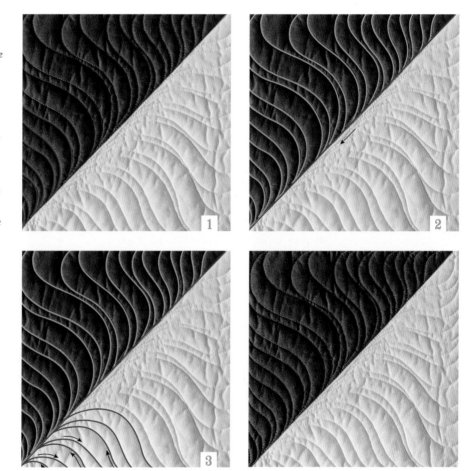

Concave Fern Feather

The Concave Fern Feather is a beautiful play on the Fern Feather (page 64). This fun design is very playful and forgiving. If you want to quilt this design on a solid block, draw a diagonal line from the lower left corner to upper right corner.

STEP 1 *Beginning in the lower left corner, stitch concave fern feathers, making sure to create a concave point at the end of each of the feathers.*

STEP 2 *Stitch an oval leaf in the top right corner, and then stitch-in-the-ditch to get back to the lower left corner.*

STEP 3 *Stitch concave fern feathers to fill in the right side of the block completely.*

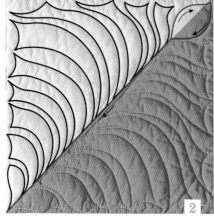
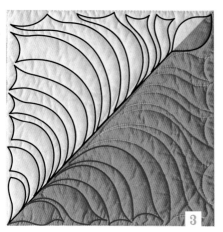

Hook Feather

The Hook Feather is a lovely yet simple way to add detail to any quilt or block. Try using half of the pattern in a setting triangle. If you want to quilt this design on a solid block, draw a diagonal line from the lower left corner to upper right corner. A hook feather is similar to a curl feather (page 12), but after you stitch to the tip of the curl, you'll leave a little space as you curl back to the spine instead of stitching over the previous stitch line.

STEP 1 *Begin by stitching hooked feathers on the left side of the block, filling in the left side of the block completely.*

STEP 2 *Stitch-in-the-ditch to get from the center of the block, from the upper right corner back to the lower left corner.*

STEP 3 *From the bottom left corner, stitch hook feathers along the right side of the block, filling in the block completely.*

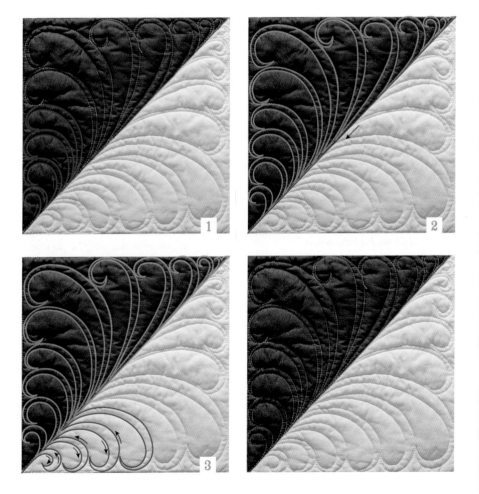

Mirrored Binary Feather

This Mirrored Binary Feather, with its little point in the corners, is a great way to modernize your quilt.

STEP 1 *Use a water-soluble marker to mark a point in the center of the block. If you want to quilt this design on a solid block, draw a diagonal line from the lower left corner to upper right corner.*

STEP 2 *Starting in the center, stitch a point feather in the center of the left side of the block.*

STEP 3 *Stitch feathers down the left side of the block. Then stitch-in-the-ditch or stitch over a marked line to get back to the center of the block.*

STEP 4 *From the center of the block, stitch feathers along the top side of the block, filling in completely.*

STEP 5 *Stitch-in-the-ditch or stitch over a marked line to get back to the center of the block. Then stitch a second point feather in the center of the right side of the block. Then fill in the rest of the block as you did on the opposite side.*

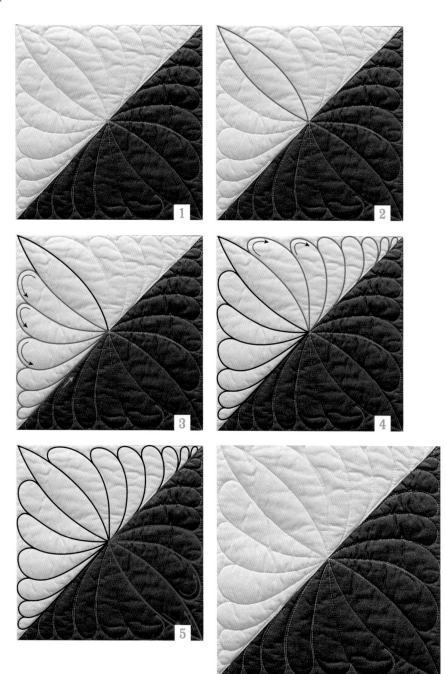

Double Half-Square Feather

The Double Half-Square Feather is shown here in a large block, yet this fun design is great for filling in smaller Flying Geese and Triangle blocks as well. If you want to quilt this design on a solid block, draw a diagonal line from the lower left corner to the upper right corner.

STEP 1 *Begin by stitching a single feather from the upper left corner to the center of the block.*

STEP 2 *Stitch a second smaller feather inside the large center feather.*

STEP 3 *Stitch a second large feather and then stitch a smaller feather inside.*

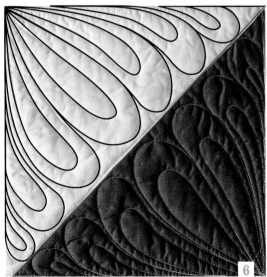

STEP 4 *Continue filling in the upper left side of the block. Then stitch-in-the-ditch back to the upper left corner.*

STEP 5 *Stitch feathers large and small, filling in the upper right half of the block.*

STEP 6 *Stitch-in-the-ditch to get from the upper right corner to the lower left corner.*

Double Half-Square Feather continued

<u>STEP 7</u> *Stitch from the lower left corner along the bottom of the block to the lower right corner. Then stitch a single large feather to the center and fill in with a smaller feather.*

<u>STEP 8</u> *Stitch in the lower right side of the block with the larger and smaller feathers and then the lower left side of block with feathers.*

Capsule Feather

The Capsule Feather is an interesting combination of feathers and figure eights.

STEP 1 *Use a water-soluble marker to mark a dot in the center of the block.*

STEP 2 *Stitch a curved line from the center of the block to a point on the lower left corner.*

STEP 3 *From the lower left corner, stitch a curved line back to the center point, then cross over in a figure-eight pattern and stitch a second curve to the upper right corner. From there stitch another curved line back to the center point.*

STEP 4 *Stitch a single feather in the center of the upper half of the block, and then stitch feathers along the left side of the block.*

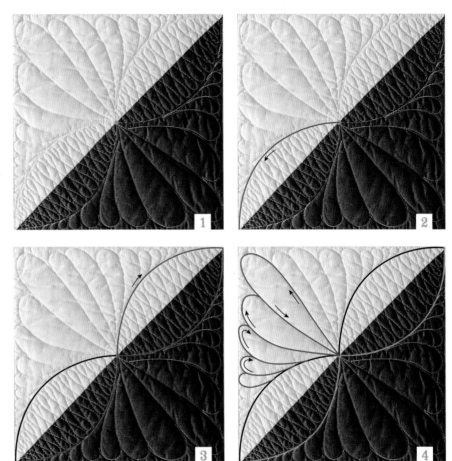

Capsule Feather continued

STEP 5 *From the lower left corner, stitch figure eights to fill in the left pod shape back to the center point.*

STEP 6 *From the center point, stitch feathers on the top right side of the block. Fill in completely to the upper right corner.*

STEP 7 *From the upper right corner, stitch figure eights to fill in the upper pod shape, moving back to the center point.*

STEP 8 *Stitch a single feather from the center point out to the lower right corner. From there continue filling feathers into the right corner.*

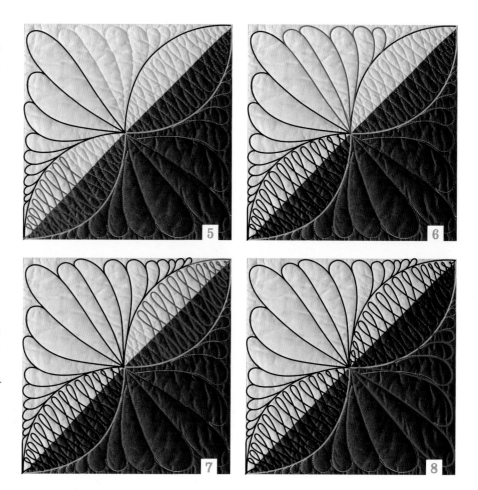

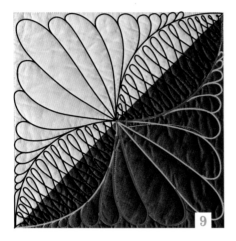

STEP 9 *Stitch along the curved line back to the center point. From that point stitch feathers to fill in the lower left side of the block.*

Chic Feather

The Chic Feather is a simple feather, yet the small opening in the spine really sets it off and adds a fun bit of detail.

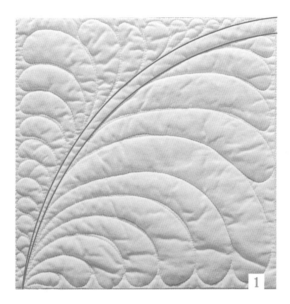

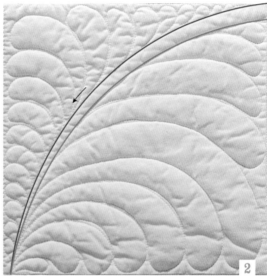

STEP 1 *Use a water-soluble marker and a curved ruler or template to draw a curved line from the upper right corner to a spot about ½˝ to the right of the lower left corner. From that same lower left corner, draw a second curved line; this time the line will end about ½˝ lower than the upper right corner.*

STEP 2 *Starting in the upper right corner, stitch along the curved line from the upper right corner to the lower left corner.*

STEP 3 *From the lower left corner, stitch feathers, filling in the left side of the block all the way to the upper right corner.*

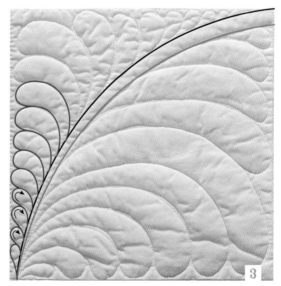

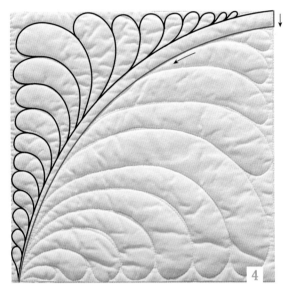

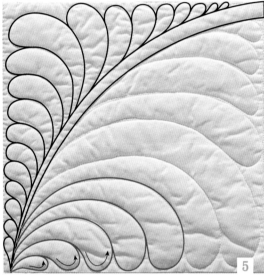

STEP 4 *From the upper right corner, stitch-in-the-ditch down about ½˝ to the lower curved line. Stitch along that line back to the lower left corner.*

STEP 5 *Stitch feathers from the lower left corner, filling in the right side of the block completely.*

Nook Feather

The Nook Feather is fun when quilted on a single block, but when paired with other blocks, this pattern creates a stunning look.

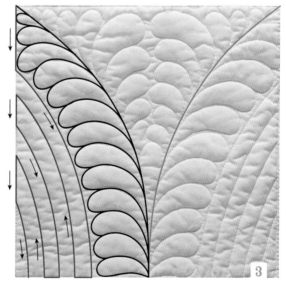

STEP 1 *Use a water-soluble marker to mark the center of the bottom edge of the block. Then use a curved ruler or template to mark a curved line from the upper left corner to the center point and then another line from the center point to the upper right corner.*

STEP 2 *Begin stitching in the upper left corner and stitch along the curved line down to the center point. From there begin stitching feathers along the left side of the curve.*

STEP 3 *From the upper left corner, stitch-in-the-ditch down the left side of the block to below the feather, and then stitch a curved line down to the bottom of the block, following the curve of the feathers. Stitch-in-the-ditch, traveling about ½˝, and then stitch an echoed curved line. Repeat this process, filling in the left side of the block.*

STEP 4 *Stitch-in-the-ditch along the bottom of the block, then travel up the center stitching line and stitch a single feather at the bottom of the V-shaped nook. Stitch feathers along the left curve line up to the upper left corner.*

STEP 5 *From the upper left corner, stitch-in-the-ditch along the top edge of the block to the upper right corner. From the upper right corner, stitch along the curved line back to the bottom center of the block, then begin to fill in feathers along the right side of the curved line. From here repeat the same process that you used on the left side of the block to fill in the right side of the block.*

Lateral Feather

The Lateral Feather is a fun design to quilt on a single block or to continue through several blocks, adding a continuous design to any quilt. If you want to quilt this design on a solid block, draw a diagonal line from the lower left corner to upper right corner.

STEP 1 *Stitch a straight line from the upper right corner through the center of the block to the lower left corner. Travel up the left ditch about ½˝ and then stitch a parallel line ½˝ away from the previous diagonal line. Travel along the top ditch about to about 2˝ from the left corner and stitch a straight line from the top of the block to the left side of the block. Travel up the ditch about ½˝ and then stitch a parallel line to the top edge of the block. Repeat this process until this section of the block is filled in completely with straight lines.*

STEP 2 *From the upper left corner, stitch-in-the-ditch down the left side of the block to the lower left corner. Pivot at the corner and stitch about ½˝ along the bottom edge of the block, then stitch a diagonal line to the upper right side of the block, ending about ½˝ down from the top right corner. Stitch-in-the-ditch along the right side of the block, traveling down to about 2˝ from the bottom right corner. Stitch a diagonal line from the right side of the block to the bottom of the block, parallel to the previous diagonal lines. Stitch over in-the-ditch about ½˝ and then turn and stitch another line parallel to the others. Continue stitching these lines until you've filled in this side of the block completely.*

STEP 3 *Stitch from the lower right corner up to the center of the larger open space. Stitch a wavy line from the upper right corner down to the bottom line, and from there begin stitching feathers along the top side of the wavy line. Fill in feathers to the right side of the block.*

STEP 4 *Stitch back down the wavy feather spine and then stitch feathers along the bottom side of the feather.*

STEP 5 *Stitch-in-the-ditch along the right side to the upper right corner, travel along the top edge of the quilt, and then stitch a wavy spine from the top down to the left edge of the block. From there use the same pattern as was used on the right side of the block to stitch feathers on one side of the spine, then stitch back down the spine and stitch the second side.*

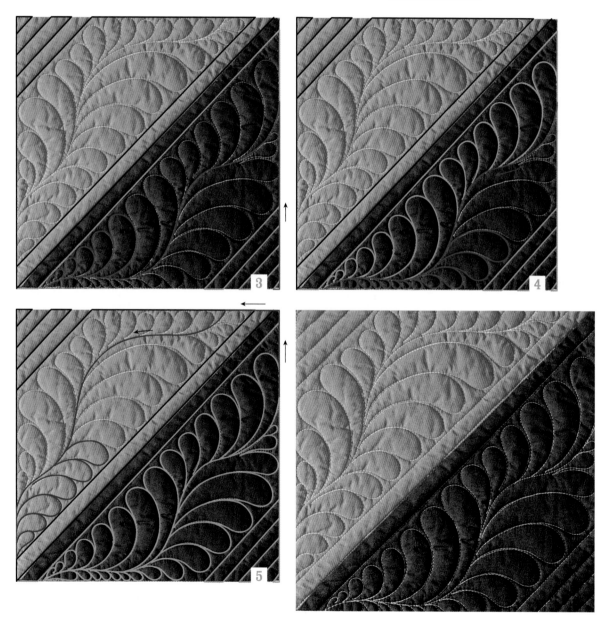

QUADRANT FEATHERS

Propeller Feather

The Propeller Feather is a fun way to add some movement to a single solid block, an Hour Glass block, or even a half-square triangle.

STEP 1 *Use a water-soluble marker to draw an X through the center of the block.*

STEP 2 *Stitch along the X from the upper right corner to the lower left corner. Stitch-in-the-ditch to the lower right corner and stitch up to the upper left corner.*

STEP 3 *Begin stitching feathers to completely fill in the left triangle shape.*

STEP 4 *Continue stitching feathers around the block, filling each of the 4 triangles completely.*

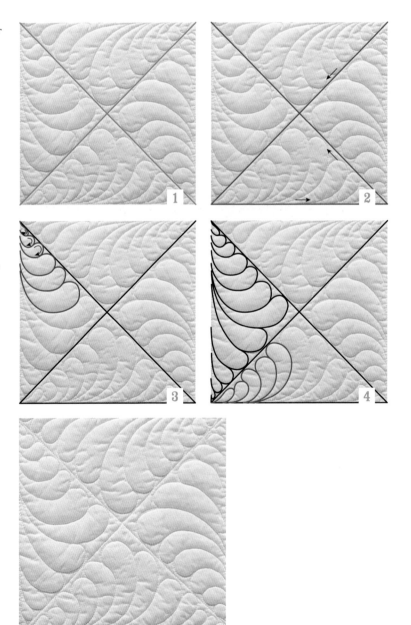

Curled Propeller Feather

The Curled Propeller Feather is a fun play on the Propeller Feather (page 80). Shown here on a half-square triangle block, the design also looks beautiful on a solid block, an Hour Glass block, or a Flying Geese block.

STEP 1 *Use a water-soluble marker to draw an X through the center of the block.*

STEP 2 *Stitch along the X, from the upper right corner to the lower left. Stitch-in-the-ditch to the lower right corner and stitch up to the upper left corner.*

STEP 3 *Begin by stitching a single feather and then a curl feather. Repeat this alternating feather pattern, filling in the left triangle completely.*

STEP 4 *Continue stitching feathers, filling in each of the triangles.*

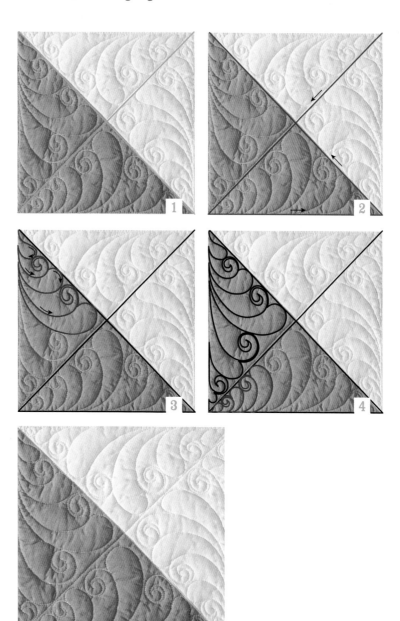

Elongated Feather

Elongated feathers are a great choice for filling in any triangle space.

STEP 1 *Use a water-soluble marker to draw an X through the center of the block.*

STEP 2 *Stitch along the X from the upper left corner to the lower right corner. Stitch-in-the-ditch to the upper right corner and stitch down to the lower left corner.*

STEP 3 *From the lower left corner, stitch a long feather, filling in from the bottom corner to the center point. Continue stitching feathers to fill in the triangle.*

STEP 4 *Stitch from the upper left corner and fill in the top triangle just as you did the side triangle. Continue filling in feathers around the block.*

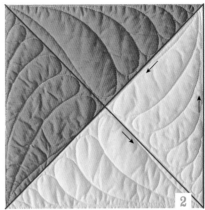

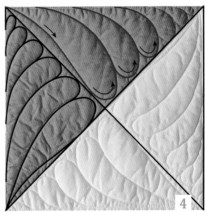

Simple Quadrant Feather

Simple quadrant feathers are fun to quilt in a solid block, as in the sample here, but they are also great fillers for Flying Geese and other pieced blocks.

STEP 1 Use a water-soluble marker to draw an X through the center of the block. Also mark a dot in the center of all four sides.

STEP 2 Beginning in the upper left corner, stitch through the center of the block on the drawn line and then travel in-the-ditch up the right side of the block to start the second diagonal line to the bottom left corner.

STEP 3 From the bottom left corner, stitch up the left ditch to the center dot. From that point stitch a center feather and then build feathers toward the bottom of the block.

STEP 4 Stitch along the ditch on the left side of the block to travel back to the center point. Then stitch feathers filling in the rest of the triangle. After you've filled in the triangle completely, travel from the upper left corner to the top center point and begin stitching feathers in the top triangle. Continue filling in feathers around the entire block.

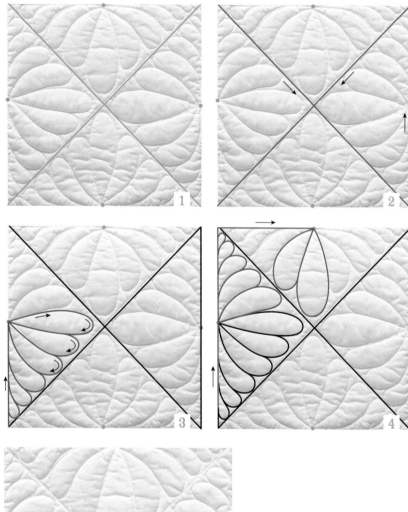

Detailed Quadrant Feather

Detailed quadrant feathers are more decorative variation of the Simple Quadrant Feather (page 83). A single quadrant fits nicely into any triangle shape.

(page 83)

STEP 1 *Use a water-soluble marker to draw an X through the center of the block and mark the center of the block on all four sides.*

STEP 2 *Starting in the upper left corner, stitch through the center of the block to the lower right corner. Stitch-in-the-ditch along the right side of the block to travel to the upper right corner. Stitch back down through the center to the lower left corner.*

STEP 3 *Stitch from the lower left corner to the center dot on the left side of the block. Stitch a single feather in the center of the triangle and then fill it in with a smaller feather.*

STEP 4 *Stitch a curl feather on the bottom side of the center feather.*

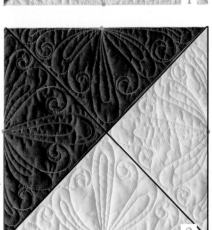

STEP 5 *Continue this pattern of alternating curl feathers with double feathers until the bottom half of the triangle is filled in.*

STEP 6 *Stitch-in-the-ditch back to the center point and then fill in the rest of the triangle with feathers. Then stitch-in-the-ditch along the top side of the block to the center point and fill in the top triangle with feathers. Use the same pattern you used in the side triangle. Continue this pattern until all 4 triangles are filled in with beautiful feathers.*

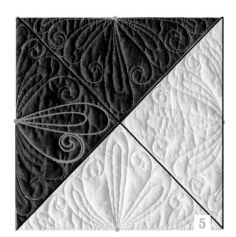

Seedling Feather

Seedling feathers are an easy quadrant feather and work well in any triangle shape

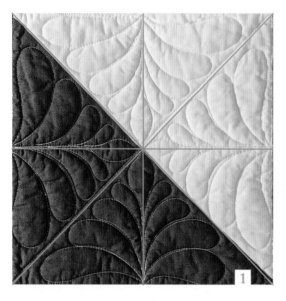

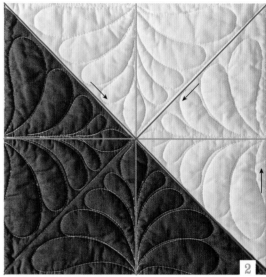

STEP 1 *Use a water-soluble marker to mark an X through the center of the block and then mark horizontal and a vertical lines through the center of the block.*

STEP 2 *Begin stitching on the upper left corner through the center of the block to the lower right corner. Travel up the ditch on the right side from the lower right corner to the upper right corner and then stitch back down the lower left corner.*

STEP 3 *From the lower left corner, stitch-in-the-ditch to the center of the left side of the block. Stitch feathers from the horizontal drawn line to the bottom of this small triangle, filling in the triangle, and then stitch a horizontal pointed feather coming back to the center of the block.*

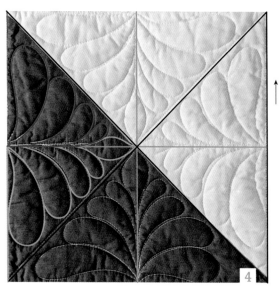
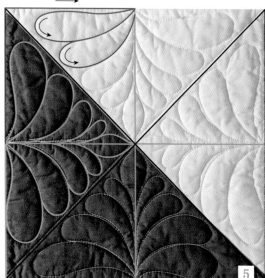

STEP 4 *Stitch back along the horizontal line to the left edge of the block and then stitch feathers on the top side of the straight line, filling in the top triangle completely.*

STEP 5 *Stitch back along the centerline to the side of the block. Stitch-in-the-ditch from the center point to the upper left corner and then across the top of the block to the center point. From there begin stitching a second Seedling Feather. Continue this process until all 4 quadrants are filled with feathers.*

Sprout Feather

The Sprout Feather is a unique feather combination. Because of the heavy stitching of the sprout, when it is stitched with contrasting thread, it really pops. When it is quilted in a thread that matches the fabric, the effect is definitely visible but more subtle.

STEP 1 _Use a water-soluble marker to mark an X through the center of the block. Then use a small curved ruler or template to mark four small sprout/seed shapes. Try to position these shapes in the center of each leg of the X._

STEP 2 _Beginning in the center of the block, stitch a center feather toward the top and then fill in feathers along the line on the left side of the triangle._

STEP 3 _Stitch down from the top left corner around the pod shape and then fill in the pod with closely spaced back-and-forth straight lines._

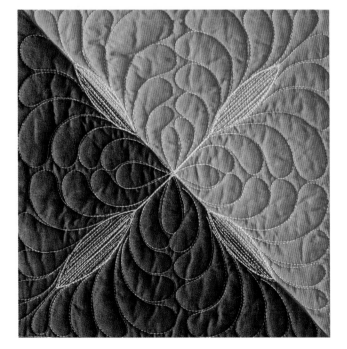

STEP 4 *Stitch back to the center and then stitch feathers, filling in the right side of the upper triangle.*

STEP 5 *Stitch down the straight drawn line and then around the pod shape. Fill it in with close back-and-forth straight lines, and then stitch back to the center. Continue stitching feathers in the right-side triangle, using the same pattern that was used in the top triangle. Then repeat this pattern in the remaining two triangles.*

Simple Sprout Feather

The Simple Sprout Feather is a great classic feather that lends itself to most patchwork blocks.

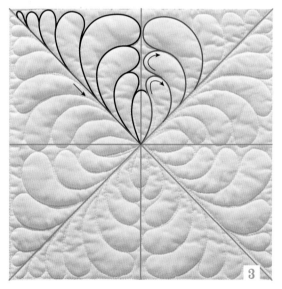

<u>STEP 1</u> *Use a water-soluble marker to mark an X through the center of the block and then mark horizontal and vertical lines through the center of the block.*

<u>STEP 2</u> *Beginning in the center of the block, stitch a single feather and then stitch up along the upper left diagonal line, filling in the triangle with feathers.*

<u>STEP 3</u> *Stitch from the upper left corner down the drawn line to the center of the block. Then stitch feathers up along the right diagonal line.*

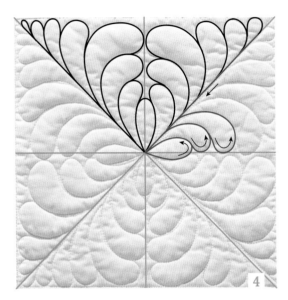

STEP 4 *Continue stitching feathers to the upper right corner and then stitch along the straight drawn line back to the center of the block. Start stitching a second set of feathers on the right side of the diagonal line. Continue stitching feathers in this same pattern filling in each triangle completely.*

FLOWER AND MEDALLION FEATHERS

Swirl Feather Flower

The Swirl Feather Flower is a lively design that nicely fills a square block.

STEP 1 *Use a water-soluble marker to mark a small circle in the center of the block.*

STEP 2 *Beginning on the left side of the circle, stitch around the circle back to the left side.*

STEP 3 *Stitch feathers around the circle, filling in the block completely.*

STEP 4 *Stitch a swirl into the center of the center circle. Stitch a small circle in the center of the swirl.*

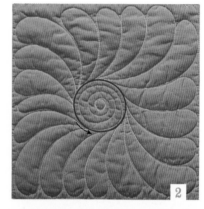

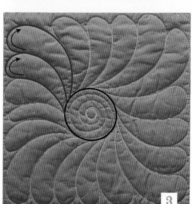

Swirl Medallion Feather

The Swirl Medallion Feather provides a lot of movement for any quilt.

STEP 1 *Use a water-soluble marker to mark a large circle in the center of the block.*

STEP 2 *Stitch a circle around the drawn line.*

STEP 3 *Stitch curl feathers around the outside of the circle, filling in the outside edges of the block completely.*

STEP 4 *Stitch a large spiral in the circle, swirl all the way into the center, and finish with a little circle right in the center.*

Sunflower Medallion Feather

The Sunflower Medallion Feather is a lively pattern that makes a feather look like a flower, perfect on any quilt you want to add flowers to.

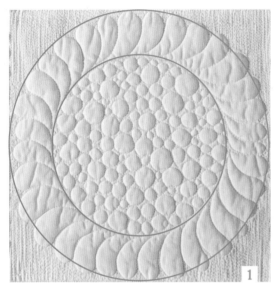

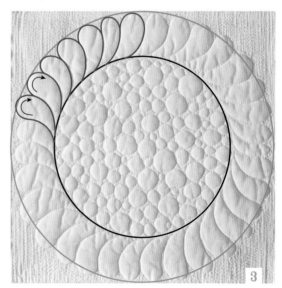

STEP 1 *Use a water-soluble marker to mark two circles in the center of the block.*

STEP 2 *Begin stitching along the smaller inner circle.*

STEP 3 *Stitch feathers around the outside of the circle, using the outer drawn circle as a reference line.*

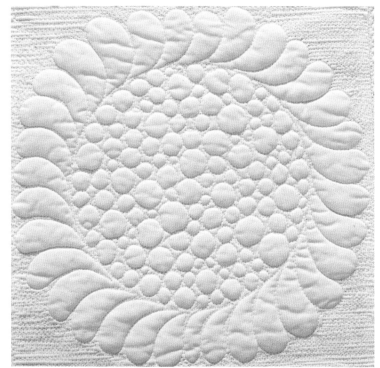

STEP 4 *Stitch pebbles in the center of the feather, filling the center in completely. I use Pebbles which is taken from* Beginner's Guide to Free-Motion Quilting *(available from Stash Books; see page 140).*

STEP 5 *Stitch close, back-and-forth straight lines on the outside of the feather circle to make the design pop.*

Modern Medallion Feather

The Modern Medallion Feather is a beautiful twist on a very traditional feather. This combination design includes feathers, pebbles, and straight lines to make a big statement.

STEP 1 Use a water-soluble marker to mark three circles in the center of the block. The two inner circles should be about ½˝ apart, and the outside circle should be about ½˝ from the outside of the block where it curves closest to the sides.

STEP 2 Stitch around the inner circle, and then stitch horizontal straight lines through the center of the circle. Stitch the lines about ½˝ apart, traveling along the circle stitch line to fill in the circle.

STEP 3 Stitch vertical straight lines about ½˝ apart through the center of the circle, filling in the circle completely.

STEP 4 Stitch circles, using an over-under pattern (over the top, then around the bottom and back over the top) between the inner stitched circle and the middle blue line.

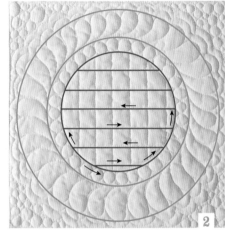

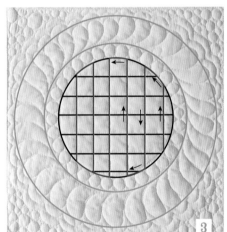

STEP 5 *Stitch along the middle blue circle and then begin stitching feathers between the center circle and the outer circle.*

STEP 6 *Stitch 2 echo lines around the outside of the ring of feathers.*

STEP 7 *Stitch pebbles in the corners outside of the outer echo line to make the feathers pop.*

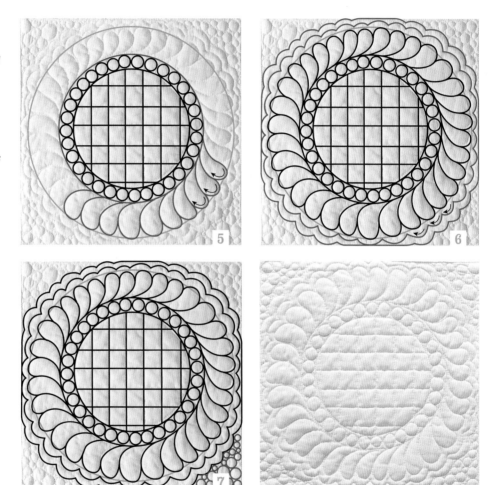

Square Medallion Feather

The closely stitched center gives the Square Medallion Feather a unique look. There will be very little negative space on the outside of the block, so this design is fabulous for most square quilt blocks.

STEP 1 *Use a water-soluble marker to draw 2 circles in the center of the block, one about ½˝ larger than the other.*

STEP 2 *Stitch the inner, smaller circle. Then fill in the inside of the circle with close back-and-forth straight lines.*

STEP 3 *Stitch around the outer circle.*

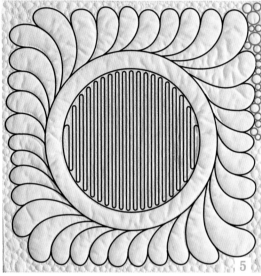

STEP 4 Stitch feathers all around the outside of the outer circle, leaving a margin of ¼″–½″ around the edge of the block.

STEP 5 Stitch tiny pebbles around the outside of the feathers to really make the feather pattern pop.

FLIRTY FEATHERS

Swirled Flirty Feather

The Swirled Flirty Feather is very forgiving, making it a great place to start practicing your feathers. This design is shown on a single solid block, but the pattern is great in the negative space of a modern quilt or even as a border design. Have fun with this playful feather design.

STEP 1 *Beginning in the lower left corner, stitch a single swirl spine with a feather on the end.*

> *tip* ◆ At this point, if you are comfortable and feel like you have good control over your machine, you can stitch back down the spine to the lower left corner. If you do not feel like you are ready to do that, simply stop, and then start stitching again in the lower left corner.

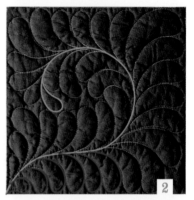

STEP 2 *At the bottom left corner, bottom of the spine, begin stitching feathers. Stitch a single feather on the right side of the spine. Continue stitching feathers on the right side of the spine, filling in the block as much as possible.*

> *tip* ◆ In making traditional feathers, you would leave about ¼" negative space between the outside of the feather and the edge of the block. Because we are making more of a modern feather, fill in the feathers all the way to the edge of the block.

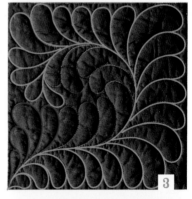

STEP 3 *Move back to the bottom left corner, or the bottom of the spine, and stitch feathers along the left side of the spine, filling in the block completely.*

> *tip* ◆ When machine quilting these modern feathers, you do not always have to make the feathers come back and touch the spine. If you look closely at this design, you will see that occasionally there are small spaces where the feather does not touch the spine, and that's okay. That's why I love these modern feathers: They are so forgiving, and yet they give your quilt a gorgeous look.

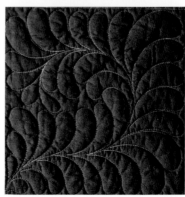

Filled Flirty Feather

The Filled Flirty Feather is shown here in a single square quilt block, but this dynamic pattern is great in the negative space of a modern quilt or even as a border design. Get creative and have fun with this playful and forgiving feather design.

STEP 1 *Beginning in the lower right corner, stitch a wavy random spine up to the upper left, and then stitch a single feather in the corner.*

STEP 2 *Stitch back down to the lower right corner and stitch a single feather. Stitch a second single feather and then fill inside along the bottom edge of the feather with smaller feathers.*

STEP 3 *Repeat this pattern, filling in every other feather with smaller feathers. After the right side of the feather is complete, move to the left side and repeat the same pattern. You may notice that I put 2 "filled" feathers next to each other on the right-hand side of the block—it wasn't intentional, but it's okay!*

SQUARE AND STRAIGHT-LINE FEATHERS

Parallel Single Feather

The Parallel Single Feather is a linear feather pattern. Shown here on just one block, this pattern could be quilted edge-to-edge on a modern or even on a traditional quilt.

<u>STEP 1</u> *Stitch parallel horizontal lines across the block every 1˝.*

<u>STEP 2</u> *Beginning in the upper left corner of the block, stitch one row of single feathers.*

<u>STEP 3</u> *After one row of feathers is complete, move to the second row and stitch a second row of feathers. Repeat this process until you have filled in the block completely.*

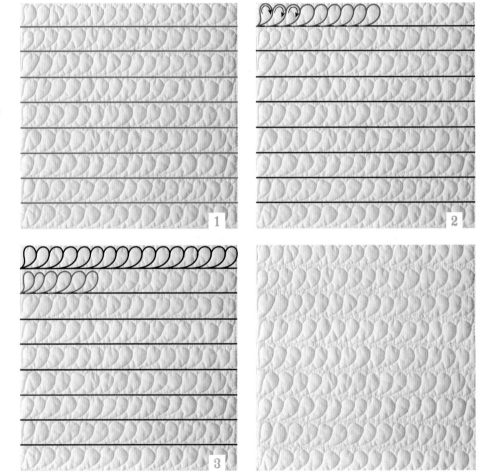

Parallel Single-Feather Corner

With the Parallel Single-Feather Corner design, the use of straight lines with single feathers adds a modern feel to a traditional feather pattern. It's perfect for corners, but why not use it as an allover design?

STEP 1 *Use a water-soluble marker to mark straight corner lines: position the first line ¼˝ in from the corner of the block and the second corner line ¼˝ in from the first line. After the completing the first two lines, draw a third line 1˝ in from the previous line. Continue drawing straight corner lines in a similar pattern until you have filled in the block completely.*

tip ◆ When I mark designs such as this, I like to use one of my rotary-cutting rulers. The marks and lines on the rulers make it easy to mark lines in any increments.

STEP 2 *Begin stitching the straight lines in the lower right corner. Stitch across, and then pivot and stitch down to the bottom of the block. Stitch-in-the-ditch over to the second drawn line. Stitch up along that line and then pivot and stitch to the right edge.*

STEP 3 *When you get back to the right side of the block, begin stitching feathers to fill in the 1˝ space, around the corner and then down to the bottom edge.*

Parallel Single-Feather Corner continued

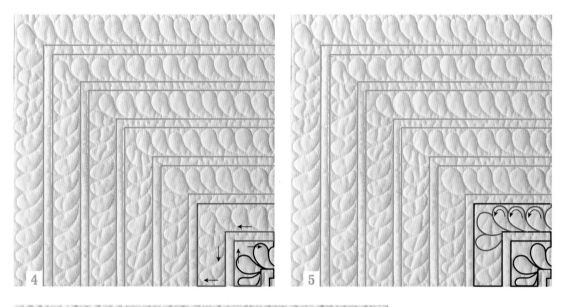

<u>STEP 4</u> *From the bottom side of the block, stitch up the straight line, pivot, and stitch to the right side of the block. Stitch back up the ditch and then stitch along the next straight line. Pivot and stitch back down to the bottom of the block. Stitch along the ditch and then stitch up the next straight line. Pivot and stitch over to the right side of the block.*

<u>STEP 5</u> *Repeat the previous steps, stitching along the straight lines and filling in the 1˝ spaces with feathers until you have stitched the block completely.*

Square Spine Feather

The Square Spine Feather gives a modern look to a traditional medallion feather.

STEP 1 *Measure the block and then divide the block in half. From there, divide the block in half again. Use these points to draw a square, using a water-soluble marker.*

STEP 2 *Begin stitching on the drawn lines. I prefer to start in the upper left corner.*

tip ◆ I generally prefer to quilt my feathers in a clockwise direction. Just as we are accustomed to reading from left to right, we also tend to be more comfortable with things that move in a clockwise direction, so stitching feathers clockwise is usually easier.

STEP 3 *Begin stitching feathers on the outside of the square spine in the upper left corner.*

STEP 4 *After you have stitched all the feathers on the outside of the spine, move to the inside and fill the inside of the square with feathers, making them almost wrap around themselves.*

tip ◆ Notice that the feathers on the outside are a bit more uniform than the feathers on the inside of the spine. Well, because you're stitching more modern feathers, that's just fine! Actually I think that it creates a bit more interest by having more playful feathers.

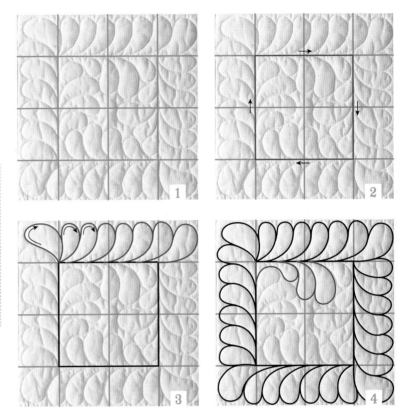

Diagonal Feather

This charming feather pattern is shown on a single solid block. This design also works well when quilted on multiple blocks going in opposite directions, in a corner, or even as an edge-to-edge design.

STEP 1 *Use a water-soluble marker to draw a diagonal line from corner to corner. From there measure out about 2˝ and mark lines every 2˝ until you have completely filled in the block.*

tip ◆ If your block is an odd size, like a 9˝ block, you may want to draw your diagonal lines 1½˝ apart instead of 2˝ apart.

STEP 2 *Beginning at the top of the block, stitch feathers on the top side of the first drawn line.*

STEP 3 *Stitch along the drawn line, and then stitch the second side of feathers on the bottom side of the first line.*

STEP 4 *Stitch-in-the-ditch down to the center straight line. Stitch along that diagonal line up to the upper right corner, and then stitch feathers on the top side of that line.*

STEP 5 *Stitch back along the centerline from the bottom left corner to the upper right corner, then stitch the feathers on the right side of the straight spine.*

STEP 6 *From the lower left corner, stitch-in-the-ditch over to the last straight line. Stitch from the bottom side of the block up to the upper right side of the block. From there stitch feathers on the top side, and then stitch back up the straight spine and stitch feathers on the right side of the spine.*

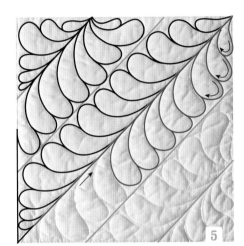 

Radiating Diagonal Feather

This fun feather pattern is shown on a single solid block. This design also works well when quilted on multiple blocks going in opposite directions, in a corner, or even as an edge-to-edge design. Another idea is to stitch this design edge to edge on a quilt but occasionally stitch full feathers and continue radiating from there.

STEP 1 *Use a water-soluble marker to mark a straight diagonal line from corner to corner. From there measure out about 2˝ and mark diagonal lines every 1½˝–2˝ until you have filled the block completely.*

STEP 2 *Beginning in the lower left corner, stitch along the straight diagonal line to the upper right corner. From there stitch feathers along the top side of the straight diagonal line.*

STEP 3 *From the lower left corner, stitch-in-the-ditch along the bottom edge to the second straight line. Stitch along that line up to the right side of the block and then up the ditch to the upper right corner. From there stitch feathers along the bottom side of the center diagonal line.*

STEP 4 *From the lower left corner, stitch-in-the-ditch back to the second drawn line. Stitch along this line for the second time, back up to the right side of the block. From the right side of the block, stitch feathers along the outside of that straight line back down to the bottom of the block.*

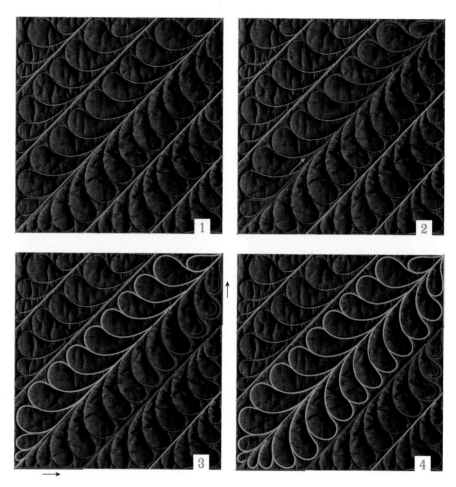

STEP 5 *From the bottom of the block. stitch-in-the-ditch over to the last diagonal line. Stitch along that line up to the right side of the block, and then fill in the bottom side of the straight spine with feathers.*

STEP 6 *Stitch from the bottom point along the ditch to the bottom left corner. From there, stitch-in-the-ditch up to the second diagonal line. Stitch along that line to the top side of the block, and then stitch feathers along the top side. From there, stitch-in-the-ditch along the left side of the block to the top diagonal line. Stitch along that line to the top of the block and then stitch feathers along the top side of that diagonal line.*

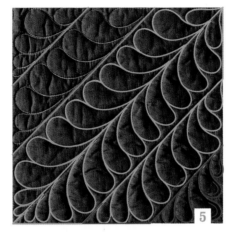
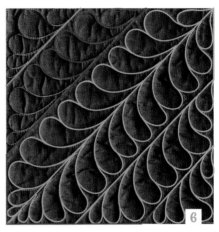
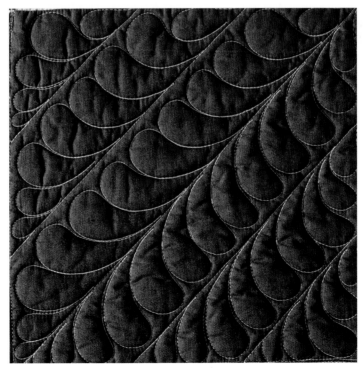

Horizontal Feather

Horizontal feathers are a fun, modern twist on traditional feathers. This design, shown on a single solid block, may also be used on a setting triangle or as an edge-to-edge design.

STEP 1 *Measure your block and then divide that measurement by four. Use a water-soluble marker to draw 3 horizontal lines spaced according to your measurement to divide the block into quarters. This block is 8˝, so here the lines are spaced 2˝ apart.*

STEP 2 *Beginning on the right side of the bottom horizontal line, stitch to the left edge of the block and then stitch feathers on the bottom side of the horizontal line.*

STEP 3 *From the right side, stitch-in-the-ditch along the right side of the block up to the center blue line. Stitch along the blue center horizontal line back to the left side. From there stitch-in-the-ditch down to the center of the bottom feather.*

STEP 4 *Stitch feathers along the top side of the bottom horizontal line. When you get to the right side of the block, stitch-in-the-ditch up to the top horizontal line. Stitch from the right side to the left side along the line.*

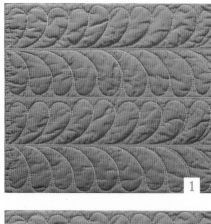
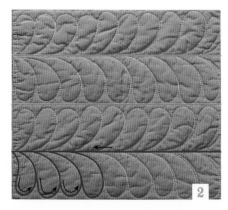
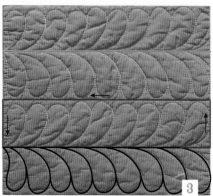
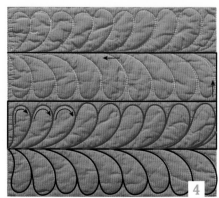

STEP 5 *Stitch feathers along the bottom side of the top horizontal line. From the right side, stitch-in-the-ditch up to the top of the block and then from right to left across the top of the block. At the top left corner, pivot and stitch down to the top horizontal line.*

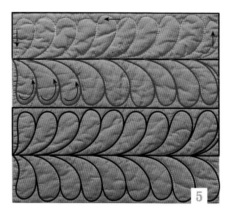 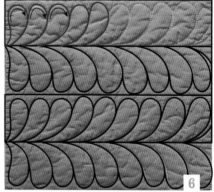

STEP 6 *Stitch feathers along the top of the top horizontal line to fill in the block completely.*

tip ◆ Make this design even more interesting by quilting with different colors of thread. For example, quilt each row of feathers in a different color, or occasionally quilt one row of feathers in a contrasting color.

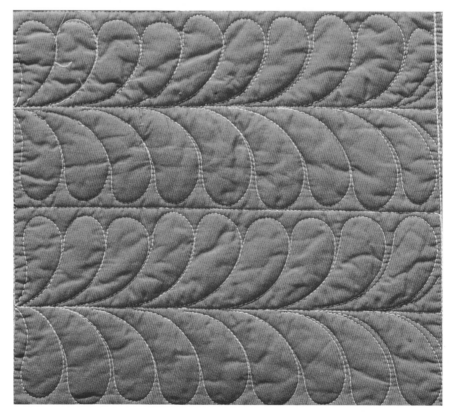

Border Block Feather

Perfect for blocks and corners, the Border Block Feather can also be enlarged and used as an edge-to-edge design on a whole quilt.

STEP 1 *Use a water-soluble marker to mark a small square 3¼˝–3½˝ in from the outside of the block. Move in about ½˝ and draw a second, smaller square. The block shown is about 12˝ square, and you may want to adjust the spacing of the squares according to your block size. If you want to quilt this design on a solid block (or any other block without a diagonal line), draw a diagonal line from the lower right corner to the upper left corner.*

STEP 2 *Beginning at the bottom right corner of the smaller square, stitch feathers on the right side of the diagonal line.*

STEP 3 *Stitch to the top of the square, filling in the right side completely, and then stitch along the diagonal line down the center of the block.*

STEP 4 *Stitch feathers on the left (bottom) side of the diagonal line.*

STEP 5 *From the upper left corner, stitch along the blue drawn line, clockwise around the smaller square.*

STEP 6 *Stitch along the diagonal line to travel from the small square out to the bigger square. Stitch around the outer square, following the blue drawn line in a clockwise direction.*

STEP 7 *Stitch along the diagonal line from the larger square to the center of the open space, and stitch a random wavy spine going in a clockwise direction around the block.*

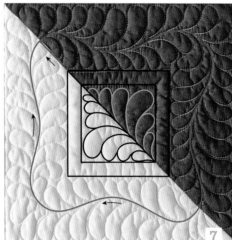

Border Block Feather continued

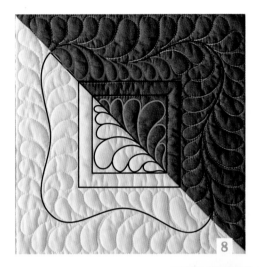 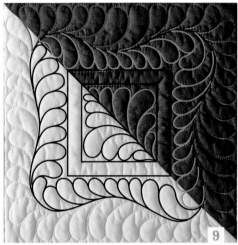

STEP 8 *Stitch feathers along the inside of the spine, going in a clockwise direction and filling in completely around the block.*

STEP 9 *Stitch feathers around the outside of the spine, filling in the outside completely.*

Half-Border Block Feather

This fun design adds a lot of interest to any block. The use of half feathers and straight lines lends a modern look.

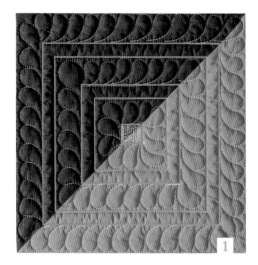

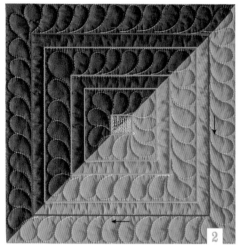

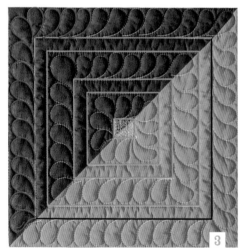

STEP 1 *Use a water-soluble marker to mark a square 1″ in from the outside edge of the block. Then move in ½″ and mark a second square. Move in 1″ and mark a third square, and then move in another ½″ and mark a fourth square. Move in 1″ more and mark a small center square. If your block is larger, continue this pattern until you have filled in the block completely.*

STEP 2 *Beginning your stitching in the lower left corner, stitch along the outer drawn blue line all the way around the outer square.*

STEP 3 *Stitch half feathers around the outside of the straight line, going in a clockwise direction.*

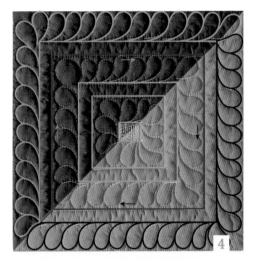

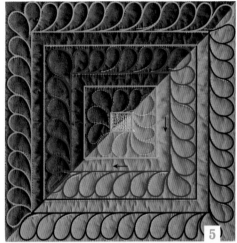

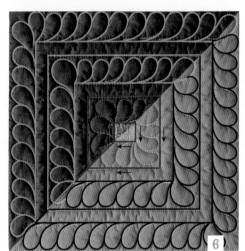

STEP 4 *Stitch a diagonal line from the corner to travel to the next inner square, and then stitch around the square, in a clockwise direction.*

STEP 5 *Stitch a diagonal line from the corner to the next inner square, and stitch around the square in a clockwise direction. Then stitch feathers in a clockwise direction around the outside of that blue line, filling in the space completely.*

STEP 6 *Stitch a diagonal line from the corner to travel to the next inner square, and stitch around the square in a clockwise direction. Then stitch a diagonal line from the corner to travel to the next smaller square and stitch around that square as well.*

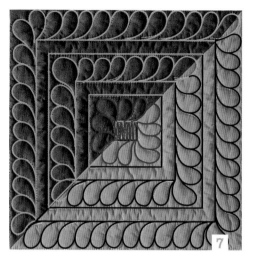

STEP 7 *Stitch feathers around the outside of the smaller square, and then fill in the smallest square with tiny back-and-forth straight lines.*

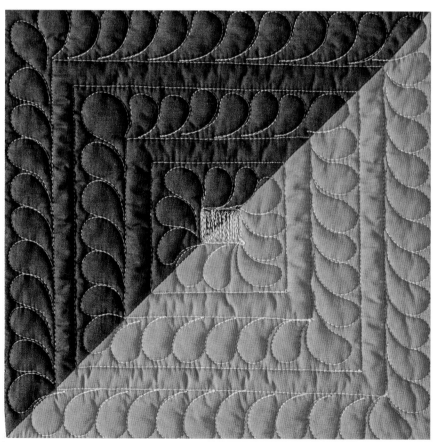

SETTING TRIANGLES OR FLYING GEESE FEATHERS

Curved Triangle

This versatile design is shown on a setting triangle and fills in the salmon-colored triangles with straight lines. The Curved Triangle design can easily be adapted and quilted in any triangle or setting-triangle block by ending the straight-line quilting as shown here at the end of the white fabric.

STEP 1 *Use a water-soluble marker and a curved ruler or template to draw 2 curved lines from the top left corner to the bottom center of the triangle and then up to the upper right corner. If there is no seamline in the middle of the block, draw a vertical line through the center of the block.*

STEP 2 *Beginning in the upper left corner, stitch along the curved line to the center point and then up to the upper right corner. From the upper right corner, stitch-in-the-ditch to the second, inner curved line. Stitch from the upper right down to the center and then back up to the upper left corner.*

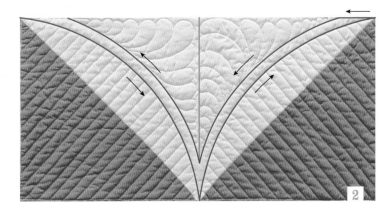

STEP 3 *From the upper left, begin stitching feathers along the inside of the curved line. Fill in completely to the center vertical line.*

STEP 4 *From the center point, stitch feathers going up the right curved line, filling in to the center vertical line.*

STEP 5 *From the upper right corner, stitch-in-the-ditch to the bottom right corner, and then across the bottom of the block to the bottom left corner. Pivot and continue up to the upper left corner. From there stitch straight lines on a 45° angle, ½" apart. Fill in this side of the block completely, and then move to the right side of the block and fill it in completely with straight lines.*

tip ◆ When stitching these straight lines, you can use a walking foot on a domestic machine. If you chose to use a free-motion foot or a longarm machine, use the markings on the ruler as your guide to keep your lines straight and all the same width apart.

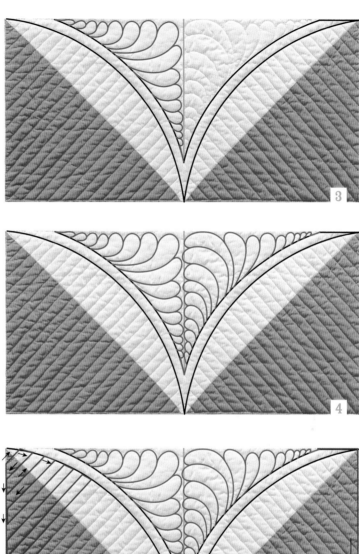

Curved Triangle continued

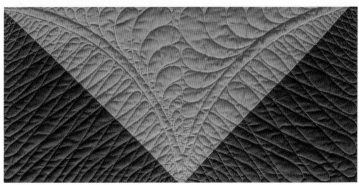

This design is quilted in the same way, but instead of stitching straight lines in the background, I've machine quilted figure eights. To add a personal touch to this design, you can quilt any filler you like where the straight lines or figure eights are.

Curved Triangle Variation

This Curved Triangle Variation is shown on a setting triangle and fills in the black-colored triangles with straight lines. This design can easily be adapted and quilted in any triangle or setting-triangle block by ending the straight-line quilting as shown at the end of the salmon fabric.

To add a personal touch to this design, you can quilt any filler you like where the straight lines are.

STEP 1 *Use a water-soluble marker and a curved ruler or template to mark two curved lines from the upper left to the center and then up to the upper right, with the inside line about ½˝ inside. If there is no seamline in the middle of the block, draw a vertical line through the center of the block.*

STEP 2 *Beginning in the upper right corner, stitch along the upper curved line down to the center point.*

STEP 3 *From the center point, stitch one feather and then build feathers upon that up the right side of the curved line.*

STEP 4 *From the upper right corner, stitch along the upper curved line down to the center point. From the center point, stitch feathers up the left side curved line. Note that this line is just a drawn line at this point and hasn't been stitched yet.*

Curved Triangle Variation continued

STEP 5 *From the upper left corner, stitch along the inside drawn line down to the center point, stopping there.*

STEP 6 *Start stitching in the upper left corner. Stitch straight lines on a 45° angle, ½˝ apart. Fill in this side of the block completely, and then move to the right side of the block and fill that in completely with straight lines.*

STEP 7 *Finish by stitching along the lower curved line from the upper right corner down to the center point and then back up to the upper left corner.*

tip ◆ When stitching these straight lines, you can use a walking foot on a domestic sewing machine. If you chose to use a free-motion foot or a longarm sewing machine, use the markings on the ruler as your guide to keep your lines straight and all the same width apart.

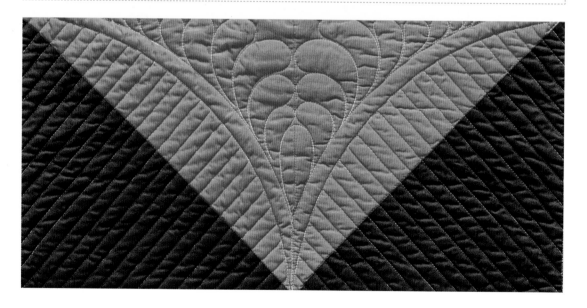

Geometric Feather

This elegant design, shown in a triangle block, is actually a setting triangle. This design is easily adapted and quilted in a corner block as well. Try it as an allover design to add modern flair.

STEP 1 *Use a water-soluble marker and a ruler to mark the first line 2˝ in from the short edges of the triangle. Mark the second and third line ¼˝ apart from the previous line. Then mark the fourth line another 2˝ inside of the previous line, followed by 2 more lines ¼˝ apart. If your block is really large, continue this pattern until you have filled in the triangle completely.*

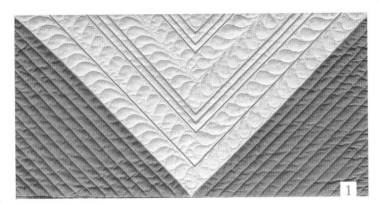

STEP 2 *Stitch a straight spine from the upper left down to the center and then up to the upper right. From there begin stitching feathers on the bottom side of the spine. Stitch from the upper right side down to the bottom and then back up the left side of the spine.*

tip ◆ Use a straight ruler to guide your stitching of the straight spine. You can draw the line with a water-soluble marker if you wish.

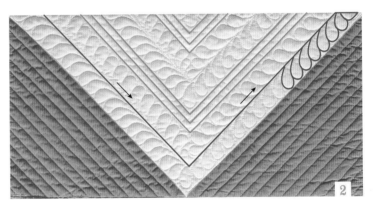

Geometric Feather continued

STEP 3 *From the upper left corner, stitch-in-the-ditch to the first drawn line. Stitch along the drawn line to the center point and then back up to the upper right side. Stitch-in-the-ditch to the first spine and then stitch feathers on the top side of the spine, from the right side to the left side of the block.*

STEP 4 *From the upper left stitch-in-the-ditch to the second drawn line. Stitch down the drawn line to the center point and then back up to the upper right side. Stitch-in-the-ditch to the third drawn line, from there down to the center, and then up to the upper left side. Again, stitch-in-the-ditch to the center of the open space. Use your ruler and stitch a straight feather spine through the center of that space to the upper right side. Then stitch feathers on the bottom side of the straight spine, filling in the bottom side completely.*

STEP 5 *From the upper left side, stitch-in-the-ditch to the fourth drawn line. Stitch along that line to the center and then back up to the upper right. Then stitch-in-the-ditch to the straight spine. Stitch feathers on the top side of the spine, filling in the space completely.*

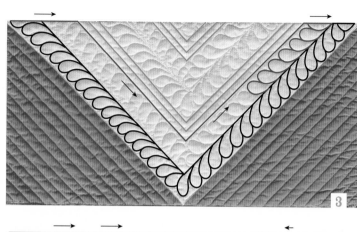

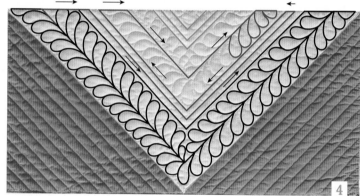

STEP 6 *From the top left side, stitch-in-the-ditch along the top edge to the fifth drawn line. Stitch along that line to the center and then back up to the right side. Then, stitch-in-the-ditch to the sixth drawn line. Stitch along that line down to the center and then up to the upper left. Stitch along the ditch and then stitch a few small feathers in the top triangle.*

tip ◆ For this design I chose to quilt straight, diagonal lines about every ½˝ in the salmon-colored fabric to really give the block a modern feel. When stitching these straight lines, you can use a walking foot on a domestic machine. If you chose to use a free-motion foot or a longarm machine, use the markings on the ruler as your guide to keep your lines straight and all the exact same width apart.

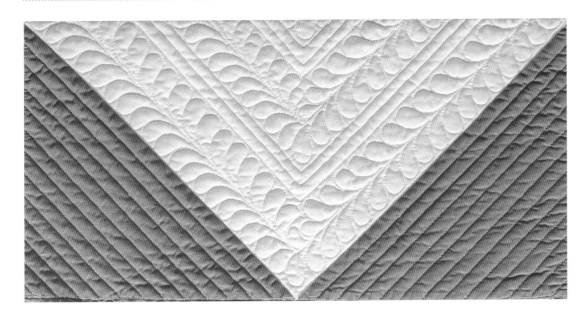

BORDERS

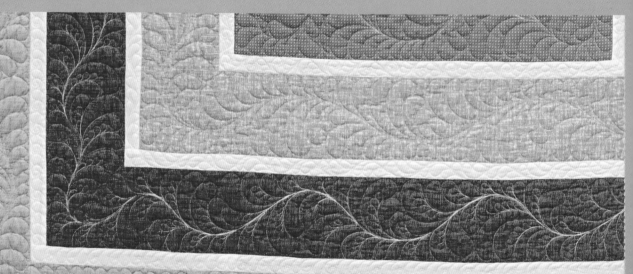

LARGE BORDERS

Straight Spine Feather

The Straight Spine Feather is an easy starting feather.

STEP 1 *Use a water-soluble marker and a ruler to mark a straight line through the center of the border you want to quilt.*

STEP 2 *Stitch along that straight line to make a straight spine.*

STEP 3 *Begin stitching on the outside of the straight spine. Stitch feathers all the way around the border.*

STEP 4 *Stitch feathers along the inside of the straight spine.*

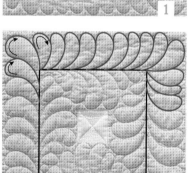

Flirty Border Feather

The Flirty Border Feather is a very playful pattern that has no rules determining the curves in the spine or the size of the feathers.

STEP 1 *Stitch a random wavy spine around the border of the quilt.*

STEP 2 *Stitch feathers around the outside of the wavy spine. This feather is very playful, so the feathers do not need to be all the same size.*

STEP 3 *Stitch feathers on the inside of the wavy spine.*

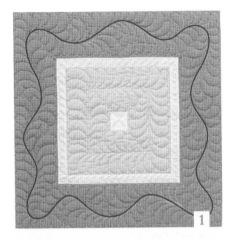

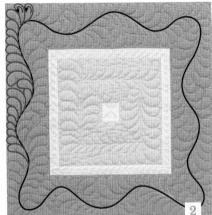

Symmetrical Feather

The Symmetrical Feather has a planned, symmetrical spine. This elegant feather is a play on a traditional feather.

STEP 1 Use a water-soluble marker and a ruler to mark a straight line through the center of the border you want to quilt with the Symmetrical Feather. Note: the following instructions work for squares.

STEP 2 Measure the length of one side of the drawn line. Divide the length by an odd number—if you want tight curves, use a larger number; if you want long, loose curves, divide it by a smaller number. The feather shown has three curves because I divided by 3. (The line is 12″ long, divided by 3 = 4″.)

STEP 3 Using the number calculated in Step 2, mark dots along each side of the square. The example shown here has 2 dots marked, dividing the line into 3 segments.

STEP 4 Using a water-soluble marker and a curved ruler or template, draw smooth, symmetrical lines through the border, making sure that the corners are convex curves, as shown.

STEP 5 Stitch along the curved spine.

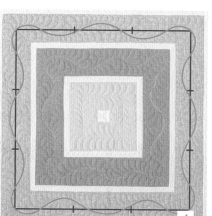

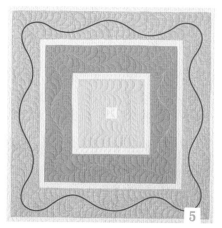

Symmetrical Feather continued

<u>STEP 6</u> *Stitch feathers around the outside of the spine.*

<u>STEP 7</u> *Stitch feathers along the inside of the spine.*

Filled Flirty Border Feather

The Filled Flirty Border Feather is perfect for larger borders— you can make the feathers a little bit bigger to fill in the space nicely.

<u>STEP 1</u> *Stitch a random wavy spine around the entire border.*

<u>STEP 2</u> *On the outside of the spine, stitch a single feather, and then fill the inside of the single feather with 3–5 smaller feathers.*

<u>STEP 3</u> *Stitch another feather. This time do not fill the inside.*

Filled Flirty Border Feather continued

STEP 4 *Stitch a third feather. This time fill in the feather with 3–5 smaller feathers. Repeat this pattern, stitching little feathers in every other feather around the outside of the spine.*

STEP 5 *Stitch on the inside of the spine following the same pattern, filling in little feathers in every other feather.*

Quad Swag Feather

The Quad Swag Feather consists of four separate feathers, one from each corner.

STEP 1 *Stitch a single feather at about the middle of the left side of the border. Then stitch a wavy spine up and around the left corner to about halfway across the top border.*

STEP 2 *In the top left corner, stitch a single feather toward the outside of the spine and a single feather toward the inside of the spine.*

STEP 3 *Stitch feathers, moving out from the left corner along the outside of the spine.*

STEP 4 *Stitch back across the spine to the left corner, and then stitch feathers on the bottom side of the feather.*

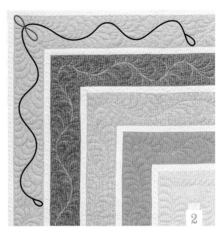

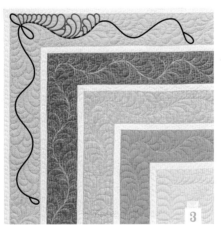

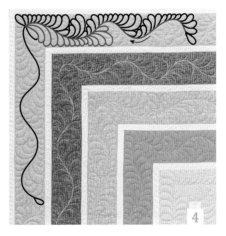

Quad Swag Feather continued

STEP 5 *Stitch back across the spine to the upper left corner, then stitch feathers down the left, on the outside of the spine.*

STEP 6 *Stitch back up the spine to the left corner, and then stitch feathers along the inside of the spine.*

STEP 7 *Stitch 4 more swag feathers in all 4 corners of the border.*

Double Swag Feather

The Double Swag Feather consists of two sets of feathers that are on opposite sides of the quilt—generally the upper left and lower right or the upper right and lower left.

STEP 1 *Beginning near the upper left corner, stitch a single feather and then stitch a wavy spine across the top of the border, around the upper right corner, and then down to the lower right corner. Stitch a second end feather at the end of the spine.*

STEP 2 *In the upper right corner, stitch a single feather toward the top outer corner and a single inner feather toward the inside of the spine.*

STEP 3 *From the center point, stitch feathers above the spine, building upon the first feather and moving toward the left side of the border.*

STEP 4 *From the left end of the border, stitch along the spine back to the right corner of the quilt, and from there stitch feathers back to the left side.*

STEP 5 *Stitch back across the spine, from the left side to the right, and then stitch feathers down the outside of the spine.*

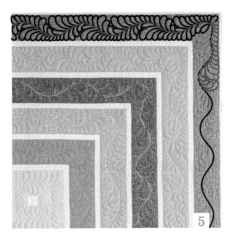

Double Swag Feather continued

STEP 6 *Stitch from the bottom of the spine to the top right corner and then stitch feathers back down the inside of the spine.*

STEP 7 *Stitch a second set of feathers, using the same pattern that you used on the upper right corner to stitch a feather on the diagonally opposite side of the quilt.*

SMALL/STOP BORDERS

Half–Hook Feather Border

The Half–Hook Feather is a beautiful little feather for a border.

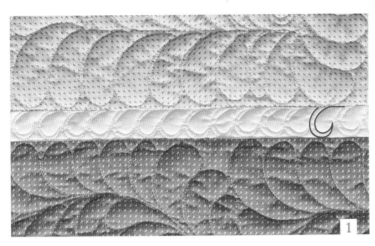

STEP 1 *Stitch a single hook feather.*

STEP 2 *Stitch a second hook feather and continue around the border.*

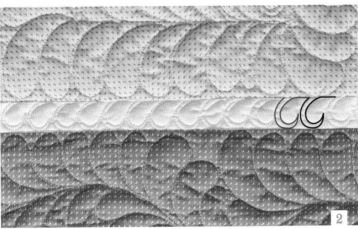

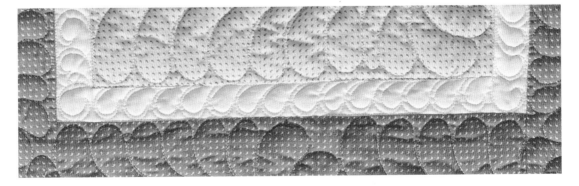

Curl Feather Border

The Curl Feather Border is a fun variation of a curl (page 12). This curl has a little feather included that is really a beautiful detail.

<u>STEP 1</u> *Stitch a single curl feather.*

<u>STEP 2</u> *Stitch a second curl feather facing the opposite direction.*

<u>STEP 3</u> *Then stitch back to the base of the second curl. Stitch 2–3 small feathers on the inside of that curl.*

<u>STEP 4</u> *Continue stitching curl feathers facing opposite directions and adding small feathers to fill in the border.*

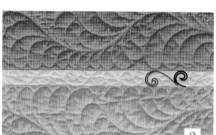

Alternating Feather Border

The Alternating Feather Border is a nice way to fill in a small border. Enlarge the pattern and use it to fill in a larger border.

STEP 1 *Stitch a single wavy spine moving from the inside to the outside of the border.*

STEP 2 *Stitch feathers to fill in the inside of the spine.*

STEP 3 *Stitch feathers to fill in the outside of the spine.*

STEP 4 *Continue this pattern, filling the border completely with feathers.*

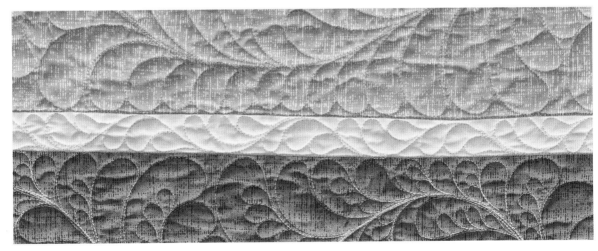

Swirl Combo Feather Border

The Swirl Combo Feather Border is a combination of the Half–Hook Feather Border (page 137) and the Half-Feather Border (page 141). Combining these two patterns creates a lovely look on almost any border.

STEP 1 Stitch a single hook feather.

STEP 2 Stitch a regular feather.

STEP 3 Stitch a hook feather.

STEP 4 Repeat this pattern, stitching regular feathers and hook feathers around the entire border.

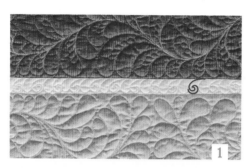

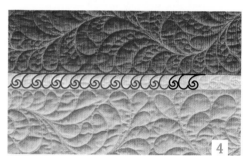

Half-Feather Border

The Half-Feather Border is a great little design to fill in a small border. This design is simple and can add just the right amount of curvature to a quilt.

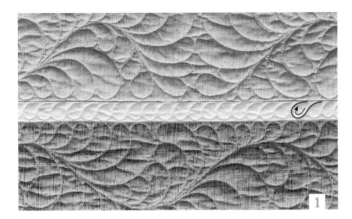

<u>STEP 1</u> *Starting on the inside of the border, stitch a single feather.*

<u>STEP 2</u> *From there stitch half feathers around the entire border.*

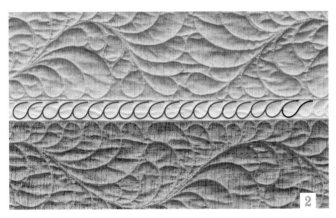

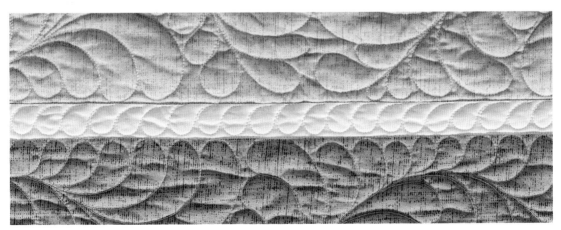

About the AUTHOR

Photo by Whitnee North

Natalia Whiting Bonner has enjoyed piecing quilt tops for more than twenty years. She learned how to quilt on her conventional home machine. She felt good about it, but she decided that if she really wanted to take her quilting to the next level, she needed to invest in a longarm machine.

In 2007, when she was pregnant with her daughter, she got the crazy idea that she should quit her job as a dental assistant and become a longarm quilter. Without really knowing what a longarm machine was, she spent a day at a longarm dealer's shop and went home having purchased a Gammill machine. Natalia's passion for quilting and being creative has grown each day since.

Shortly after her purchase, Natalia began blogging at pieceandquilt.com, and blogging became her connection with other quilters and fellow work-at-home moms. By 2009 her quilting business had grown, and it was time to leave the tiny, poorly lit bedroom where she had been doing all her quilting. Natalia moved into a studio at her parents' home, and with the inspiration of her mother, Kathleen Whiting, she has realized that the sky is the limit. Natalia has since moved her studio again, to her home this time, where she can work with her children at home with her.

Whether it's working on an intense show quilt or a simple baby quilt, Natalia has become a total quilting addict. She has won numerous awards for her work. She has been featured on Moda Bake Shop and in *Quiltmaker Magazine, Fons and Porter Magazine* and *American Patchwork and Quilting Magazine*, and she has contributed to *Fresh Fabric Treats, Modern Blocks*, and *Sweet Celebrations with the Moda Bake Shop Chefs*. Natalia's first Craftsy class debuted in September 2016.

Also by Natalia Bonner:

Want even more creative content?

Make it, snap it, share it *using* *#ctpublishing*